THE GENTLE ART OF LISTENING

Counselling Skills for Volunteers

Janet K. Ford grew up in North Yorkshire. She was a student in Oxford, Leeds and Lancaster and has degrees in Social Psychology and Religious Studies.

After a number of years in the Health Service she developed an interest in community work. Since 1987 she has worked for Victim Support as a co-ordinator. Her experience of training volunteers comes from work with both Victim Support and Samaritans at local and national levels.

Janet K. Ford is a member of the British Association for Counselling and is on the executive committee of her local council for voluntary service. She has made her home in Lancaster.

Philippa Merriman began her professional career in the late 1960s teaching philosophy. By the early 1970s she had joined the Probation Service and, after a prison secondment, pursued her research interest in social administration, producing work on the families of long-term prisoners in the United States. From this she developed an interest in working with both professionals and volunteers in statutory and voluntary agencies. By the early 1980s she was involved in the training of Victim Support volunteers and professional social workers.

She lives in Lancaster and is a social work tutor at Lancaster University.

THE GENTLE ART OF LISTENING

Counselling Skills for Volunteers

Janet K. Ford and Philippa Merriman

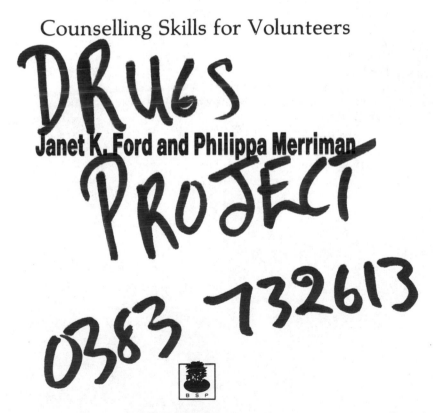

DRUGS

PROJECT

0383 732613

Bedford Square Press

Published by
BEDFORD SQUARE PRESS of the
National Council for Voluntary Organisations
26 Bedford Square, London WC1B 3HU

First published 1990

Typeset by A.K.M. Associates, Southall, London.
Printed and bound in Great Britain by
J.W. Arrowsmith & Co, Bristol

British Library Cataloguing in Publication Data
Ford, Janet
    The gentle art of listening :
    counselling skills for volunteers. — (survival handbooks)
    1. Counselling
    I. Title   II. Merriman, Philippa   III. Series
    361.323

    ISBN 0-7199-1283-0

Contents

For D. W. Amibar, who was born on a most beautiful weekend.

Preface

Becoming a volunteer in a counselling and/or befriending
capacity is not a decision to take lightly. Being a volunteer is
sometimes rewarding and enjoyable, sometimes difficult.
Training people to be volunteers can be anxiety-provoking
because it involves asking many questions for which there are
no easy answers. The process of exploring those questions is
exciting but can lead to uncertainty, where volunteers wonder
whether they can ever be of any use to any client.

This book has been prepared with a view to helping
volunteers ask themselves very precise questions in a number
of clearly defined areas. The hope is that by committing some
answers to paper volunteers will have a sense of having
contributed to their own training by arriving at answers which
will work for them.

We therefore ask you to read this book with a pen in your
hand, ready to write down your thoughts, opinions, feelings
and judgements. You can be confident that your answers are
as good as anyone else's, and far more significant in this
context, since ultimately it is you that your clients will be
relating to. Write down your first thoughts as you read the
book – then write down your second thoughts later.
Comparing them can be a useful exercise.

The preparation of this book has been stimulating and
thought-provoking for both of us. We would like to thank
Shelley Neiderbach in particular for her systematic criticism
and encouragement, and all the other people who provided us
with the time and space in which to write this book.

JANET K. FORD
PHILIPPA MERRIMAN

1 Being a volunteer

Introduction

This book is for volunteers and anyone else who is thinking of working in situations which involve offering emotional support. We aim to look at what can be involved in befriending and counselling in a voluntary capacity and at how to prepare for this. The thinking behind our approach is that if you are interested in the work and can see the point in doing it, then you probably already have what it takes to do it well. We hope to help you sort out what it is about you that is useful and important to other people. Understanding this means that you can clarify how well you are doing your job and how to make sure that you look after not only your client and the organisation you belong to, but yourself too.

We do not aim to offer too many suggestions about what you should or should not say, or about what you should or should not do. What we do suggest is the type of questions you should consider and the issues you should have thought about. We hope that by encouraging you to clarify some major uncertainties you can approach the work with the confidence that you know what you are doing. You should also know why you are doing it, and how well.

We hope, too, that by following the way this book works, and by answering the questions it asks, you will come to accept your own strengths and limitations. We suggest that you write down your answers to the questions as you go along and have them there to refer back to. There are no right answers and you may find that, over time, you have new answers when you go back to the old questions. That in itself will tell you something about how you are working and how the work is affecting you.

Throughout the book we shall refer to the volunteer as female and, with one exception ('Caring for the carers' in chapter 5), the client as male. This is because by far the larger proportion of voluntary workers are women, at least in the United Kingdom. We are not suggesting that this is the way it ought to be; we simply acknowledge that this is the way it is. What follows, however, is equally relevant to male volunteers. Although it may not be the case that the majority of clients are in fact male, we have spoken of them as though they are in order to avoid ambiguity in some of our examples. Perhaps we should also say why we have chosen the word 'client'. Quite simply, it seemed the most appropriate term. Your organisation will probably refer to the people who use its services in particular terms. The word 'client' seems to us to cover all eventualities. It includes customers, callers, patients, victims and users and is one that will be commonly understood by the people with whom you work.

Getting launched

When thinking about important decisions like changing jobs or less important ones like joining a club, there are probably four types of question we ask ourselves:
1 Why, and how much, do I want to do this?
2 How much time am I prepared to spend on this new job/club?
3 Do I have the information or skills I shall need to do well?
4 Do I have the aptitude and interest to come by those skills and areas of information which I do not already possess?

This book assumes that, as a volunteer, you will have considered what you are committing yourself to in a way rather similar to the way you might consider applying for any other job. We assume you will have asked yourself what the organisation does and how its values reflect your own. You will also presumably have established what the job of the volunteer is within the organisation. You will know how well you are equipped for the tasks involved in terms of your temperament, abilities and past experience. We also assume that you will have made some decision about how interested you are in acquiring the other skills you will need. You will have decided how many hours a week or a month you are prepared to make available for voluntary work and how these will be spread out. Presumably you will have taken into account your family and friends, who may be affected by your decisions.

But behind these apparently straightforward questions there are other, more difficult ones. Although you may be quite clear that the work of the Samaritans or Relate impresses you as worthwhile, you may not be confident that you can offer what is needed. You will meet clients who are depressed or lonely or who are experiencing marital discord, for example. 'Wanting to help people' and 'getting on with people' sound inadequate and weak descriptions of yourself as somebody who may be able to help. Filling those ideas out in a way which pinpoints exactly what you need to do may be difficult. It is not always easy to establish the best way of preparing yourself for a new task, especially when it may not be clear to you how working in this sphere will affect you.

In chapters 2 to 7 we make a number of suggestions to help you answer the difficult questions which lurk behind the straightforward ones. The answers are up to you. The important thing is that they are your answers, the ones which will work for you. They are the ones which will make sense to you and to your clients. We stress again that the answers will not be the same for everyone and the ones you give do not always have to stay the same.

Counselling and befriending

In chapter 2 you will be invited to explore the capacity which is absolutely crucial in counselling – the ability to listen. This is not the same as the listening we do when the radio is on or when we listen out for the postman. It is the sort of listening which establishes a relationship between you and the person you are listening to. It is the sort of listening which helps the person who is talking decide what he can say to you. It involves the ability to put yourself in other people's shoes and understand at least something about the way they feel. This is important because at the very root of all counselling and befriending is the idea that people – we – all benefit from knowing that other people are interested in us and understand us.

We rarely want other people to understand *everything* about us but most of us, most of the time, feel better for discovering that someone is on the same wavelength and that we are not alone. Sometimes, even, we do not expect people to understand us and do not resent it if they find this difficult. There are, after all, times when the whole point of talking is to try to make sense of something for ourselves by explaining it. It is often only through the process of finding the right words to explain how we feel that we come to realise these feelings ourselves.

Although it is gratifying if the person we explain such things to seems to understand, it is most important that he or she gives undivided attention. For most of us it is a help to know that at least one person thinks that we and our concerns are important enough to give time to. It is the sort of attention which is perhaps the most valuable part of counselling. Listening in the sense we are talking about means paying attention to everything that a client is expressing either in words or in other ways and to nothing else.

Why do you do it?

Sometimes we need people to understand us because we want them to do something; sometimes we just need to know that someone is interested enough to take the trouble to understand. Those are often the very times when it is hardest to believe that anyone is, or can be, interested in us. At times when our own confidence is low and our trust in other people and the world is shaken, we wonder if other people are really interested or really understand. That is why it is important for you, the volunteer, to be able to answer, for both yourself and your client, what it is that you get out of the work you are doing. How do you answer the client who asks whether you are really interested in him, and why?

It is necessary to work out how you can explain your interest, rather than simply to express it by your behaviour. But it is also necessary to be able to think about the way you listen and see how this can be helpful to your client and how, by listening better, you can be more helpful. We ask you to think about what your organisation can offer best and about whether you are actually listening to this client rather than hearing what you expect people like him to say. We hope that by spending some time thinking about, and writing down, some of the ways you view people and their problems you will become a little more aware of your own attitudes and therefore of the ways your clients are likely to see you.

At the same time that this book invites you to think about what is involved in listening and the purpose behind it, there are also invitations to look at what, as a befriender, you are *not* doing. We ask you to consider what you can and cannot, should and should not, do for people. Whichever organisation you belong to there will be limits to the nature of your work and the service it is appropriate and possible for you to provide. There are going to be some things you should not and cannot do. However much you want to and however badly these things are needed, they are not your job. Facing this will lead to some consideration of how you feel when you cannot meet what you and your clients see as their needs.

Your clients' feelings and your own

By the very nature of the help you are offering, much of your concerns will be with other people's feelings. Therefore, you will often find your own feelings becoming involved. For this reason it is important for you to be able to draw very clear lines, so that both you and your client know where your work ends and where your personal life begins. This, however, is easier said than done.

While it is the client's concerns, anger and fear that may be the focus of your attention, it would be strange indeed if he could express all these to you without there being any repercussions for your own emotional life. We invite you to look, therefore, at how well you recognise your own emotional needs and limitations. We point out that it is important to discover whether there is anyone in your organisation who can help you sort out your own feelings. We provide you with the opportunity to think about how your work affects your own life, what you do about this, and how you decide where and when to draw the line.

Knowing more about yourself

In chapter 5, for example, we ask whether you are frightened or angered by other people's feelings. Having involved your own feelings in order to understand your client's, can you still keep your feelings separate from his and recognise if you are getting over-involved? The fact is that what you are listening to are your client's problems – not yours. If you are to do your job well you must remember this and work out what stance you need to adopt to regain your composure should you have a particularly difficult time with a client.

Obviously it is difficult to know answers to these types of question in advance, when there are no particular situations in mind. But it is even harder not to lose a sense of perspective and find yourself overwhelmed in a particularly taxing situation if you have not at least thought about the relevant questions to ask beforehand. Behind our comments is the idea that you will work better if you know a little more, not just about the job but about yourself.

With this in mind we stress the importance of being able to see parts of ourselves in parts of our clients. It is after all only by recognising that our clients' behaviour and feelings are much like our own might be in some circumstances that we can understand much of what we are told. But by the same token we invite you to consider that you, like your clients, have emotional needs and from time to time need emotional outlets. It would be foolhardy, and perhaps a little arrogant to invite clients to express or discuss their feelings while denying our own needs in this direction. All too often, as volunteers, we fail to notice that we are not behaving to clients as we behave to ourselves, or as we would expect other people to behave to us. We offer emotional support to our clients and neglect ourselves.

In the chapters to come, therefore, we invite you to think about whether you know your limitations. Can you talk about your feelings in the same sort of way you expect your client to, or is there something in you that tries to deal with feelings along the lines of 'don't worry about me, I'll be all right'? We invite you to think about whether you are prepared to give yourself the same consideration which you are prepared to give to your clients.

Where to draw the line

Right at the beginning of this chapter we suggested that when you decided to get involved you probably laid down some guidelines about what you were prepared to get involved in and how much time and energy you were prepared to invest. That would, at least, be a good start. But there are other lines that you need to think about drawing. From time to time you may want to rub these lines out and draw them somewhere else as you and your own situation change. The important thing is that there always are some limits. It is very easy, otherwise, to be taken over by situations and this may well not be in the best interest of either you or your client.

We look, for instance, at how to draw the lines involved in deciding who your clients actually are. Do you work with the individual who is referred to you; him and his family or him and his friends? Clearly there can be no one answer to a question like this, but at least we suggest some ways to arrive at a sensible and appropriate decision on any particular occasion. More to the point, we suggest that it is important for you to explain what your decision is to your client. That way both of you understand and accept the basis of your relationship and the reasons behind the time you spend together.

Drawing up contracts

Identifying your client is part of the more general consideration which we highlight by asking the question: what would be in a contract between you and your client? The answer to a question of that sort will take into account not just who is going to be involved, but how often, when, where and to what purpose. In other words, there will be space in this book for you to establish a few of the more important boundaries in connection with your involvement. For example, what exactly is your job? What is not your job? What are you good at? What are you not good at? How is the work to be divided up between you, your client and other people who may be involved with him?

Working with professionals

Having decided who the client is and what the job is, it still remains to look at who else is involved and where the volunteer stands in relation to the organisation of which she is a member. For this reason we devote a chapter to looking at some of the questions relating to working with professionals and working within an organisation. Unless the volunteer is clear where she stands, both of these can lead to difficult situations for her.

It is worth considering, for instance, how far you are aiming at the same ends as the professionals involved. In many cases you may be working towards the same end, especially if you are working for the same organisation. But this will not always be the case. Sometimes you and a professional worker may be in contact with the same client for entirely different reasons. In this event you will need to consider how far what you are doing fits in with what the professional is doing. You may also find it useful to look at how far you share the same values and how far your strengths differ from those of other people working with your client.

Authority, responsibility and confidentiality

You will also need to think about the question of authority.
Like most professional workers, you will be responsible for a
particular task or area of work, and accountable to someone
within an organisation. We invite you to look at what the
limits of your responsibility are and where, therefore, your
authority lies. Because of what your organisation does, and
because of your job within it, you will have some authority. An
important part of what you do will depend on how you see
that authority and how you act on it in the best interests of
your client.

Similarly, the service you give to your clients is likely to be
affected by your view of how much information you should
disclose and to whom you should disclose it. We assume that,
all other things being equal, your client is entitled to complete
confidentiality. Sometimes, though, all other things are not
equal. There will be times when it may be appropriate to pass
on information to someone with different responsibilities and
a different area of authority. We suggest the issues you need
to consider to be able to provide yourself with some clear-cut
lines. That way you can work with the confidence that you are
neither neglecting your responsibilities nor overstepping the
mark.

Working with special groups

We hope that no matter what organisation you work in there
will be something in the book for you. However, we do
recognise that special talents and particular approaches are
called for when dealing with certain client groups. Since a large
number of voluntary organisations are concerned with
providing physical and material support for their clients in
addition to emotional help, we have included a chapter on
health problems.

We investigate some connections between physical and
emotional distress. In particular, it is recognised that there is a
great deal of important work for a volunteer to undertake with
clients who are physically or mentally ill or who are facing
death. The strains and tensions often associated with such
circumstances can lead anyone to behave in an inappropriate
way. If, as a volunteer, you are not clear what the most
appropriate response is, the client may not be served as well as
anyone would wish.

Likewise, the awareness of possible pain, disfigurement or

disablement is something that tends to create considerable anxiety for many of us. It may well be that seeing somebody else in such a situation arouses feelings in us which make us less than helpful to him. Once again we invite you to think in advance what your anxieties are and how you can best deal with them, because it is important that your responses to your client and his family reflect their needs rather than your own difficulties with your feelings.

Another section looks at some aspects of physical ill-health and mental ill-health in a way which will make it possible for you to offer the right sort of support, not only to the person who is ill, but to the people who are most closely involved in caring for him. Your own responses to the prospect of ill health may give you at least some insight into the feelings of those who are the carers. It is also appropriate to consider the support you may be able to offer when you are involved with a client who is dying.

In the section about death we offer some suggestions which may help you clarify what the issues may be for your client and what they are likely to be for those who are close to him. Ultimately you may need to transfer the focus of your attention away from the person who is dying and towards those who will survive him. We hope to make you sensitive to some of the issues involved.

Things that can go wrong

We assume that, for most of the time, you and your clients understand each other and work well together. Your clients find contact with you useful and valuable and you derive some satisfaction from knowing that you are doing your job well. Sometimes, though, things do not seem to go right. In chapter 6 we list a number of the most common areas where things can go wrong and suggest ways of coping with them. At the very least you can take comfort from the fact that when the circumstances we describe happen to you, you are by no means the first.

First, practicalities such as when, where, and how often to meet are considered. The implications of home or office visits or of meeting on neutral territory are clearly different. These details will set the scene in a way which will probably affect what happens in the meeting. In view of this it clearly matters who is in control of the decisions about how arrangements are made.

Second, what happens between you and your clients will

depend not only on what is on his mind but on your frame of mind, too. If you are preoccupied, your client will miss your undivided attention. We suggest ways of reducing your anxieties so that you are free to give your client the attention he needs and expects. We point out that there are alternatives available to you if your own state of mind is likely to intrude into your time with the client.

Getting the meeting place right depends on both you and your client, and getting your own frame of mind right depends entirely on you. The third area to be looked at involves situations where something goes wrong between what is going on in the client and the way you understand him. As examples we look at transference and projection. Here everything is far from straightforward. In the first case the client is dealing with his feelings in a roundabout way by making you the object of emotions that should really be directed elsewhere. In the second case the client makes assumptions about your feelings and reactions which are not, in fact, accurate. We hope to alert you to the fact that these things happen so that once you recognise the situation you can respond to it appropriately.

While transference and projection occur unconsciously on the part of clients, this is not always the case with the fourth area we consider. This is manipulation. Your client may involve himself in fantasy or lying in an attempt to elicit the emotional responses he needs. He may become verbally or physically abusive to try to make you act in the way he wants. In each of these cases you need to be aware of what is happening and why. Then you need to make up your mind what would be in your client's best interests and when you need to start looking after your own. Getting it right may be different in different circumstances, but it can be done.

The fifth area to be discussed involves physical contact. Once again, it is not possible to lay down hard and fast rules. We suggest some considerations which need taking into account when, as a volunteer, you think of communicating your support in this particularly direct way.

Finally, brief space is devoted to the infrequent circumstance where the relationship between volunteer and client breaks down. Sometimes personalities clash and sometimes situations are too painful or difficult. Even in these cases it is important that both the volunteer and the client leave the relationship with their self-confidence and self-esteem intact. Once again, it is not easy, but it can be done.

Knowing when to stop

When you get to the point where the work that you do is taking more out of yourself than it is giving to the client, it is time to stop. The question is, how do you know when that point has come? We look at ways of distinguishing between what is passing tiredness and the first indications that a more major change is called for. It is argued that if you do not look after yourself, then the sheer amount of work which you do may finally get to you. Your zest for the job will diminish and you will become less effective.

For this reason we look at ways of deciding when to take a break or perhaps thinking that longer-term action is called for. It does not make sense to give your client more consideration than you would give yourself, and we invite you to look at your own needs in a way similar to that in which you would assess those of any client. There is a case for arguing that you are your own most important client.

We will also be looking at what it means to have been a volunteer – how do you let go of the things that were important to you and gave you a sense of fulfilment? How do you deal with the sense of regret at leaving?

Through the book we shall concentrate on many of the worst possible situations and, in reading it, you may wonder why on earth anyone should volunteer to put themselves in such situations. We are relying on the fact that you yourself will know how thoroughly enjoyable spending time with people you might not otherwise meet can be. You should also be getting a sense of satisfaction and fulfilment from the work you do. If you are not, we hope this book will help you discover, or rediscover, all the positive benefits of being a volunteer.

2 Listening skills

Active listening is a skill

Listening is something that we all do at some time, so why the need to think of it in terms of skills? The listening that we are considering in this chapter is that which involves you as an active participant. When listening to the radio, your mother, the greengrocer, you can choose whether you are going to involve yourself on a level other than that of passive hearer. But if you involve yourself on a deeper level, as you would with a client, then your listening needs to become 'active', a positive input into the relationship between you.

Your listening, therefore, must have some reason for being, some aim and intent, and some limitations. It must involve more of you than just your ears, but not involve so much of you that your whole life revolves around the people you listen to, whether for good or bad. You must know what you are doing, why you are doing it, and the possible effects on both the client and yourself.

Whatever kind of voluntary work you are doing, so long as it involves clients, you are putting yourself in a position where you are wanting him (the client) to make use of you. To some extent the title and aims of your group, i.e. Age Concern, Samaritans, Citizens Advice Bureau, provide sufficient reason for someone to talk to you. But he is talking to *you*, with all your individuality, body language, loose dentures, red hair and so on, not some faceless organisation. So when he asks you, 'Why are *you* listening to me, why are *you* caring about me, why are *you* prepared to give up your time for me?' you need to have worked those things out for yourself beforehand.

Be honest with yourself

Just because you are in a position of hoping to be able to give
something to your client, and he has come to you because he
hopes to receive something from you, it does not make him
any less perceptive. If your main reason for being there is
because the work will look good on your curriculum vitae or
because it gets you out of the house for a couple of hours a
week, it will affect and limit the quality of the relationship
between you and your client. If you could not tell your client
the real reasons for your involvement with the work, then you
should question what you are doing.

Being honest with yourself will probably involve
acknowledging that your interest in the work that you do is
primarily, although not exclusively, because of your own
needs. Far from being a selfish, self-centred way of thinking, it
means that you realise that you are getting something out of
the work you do not only for the client but also for yourself. If
this were not the case you would soon reach a state of burn-
out. You would have given all you are capable of giving and
would have to go off somewhere else to have your own needs
answered. Most of us have a need to be needed; if you can find
the resolution of part of this need in the work that you do
with other people who have additional needs, then you will be
starting from a mature and stable basis.

How you express this to the client is something only *you* can
work out. To say to him 'I am here because it makes me feel
good' smacks of voyeurism and is hopefully not true. You are
with that particular client because he has some particular
problem or need. It may be distressing for both of you to listen
as he expresses it. So you must be able to explain why your
general involvement in the work that you do has brought you
to this particular time and place with him.

Issues to think about

- What do you get out of the work that you do?
- How do you explain that to a)a friend, b)a colleague, c)a client?
- If you were the client and the volunteer was not able to
  answer the question 'Why me?', what feelings would you
have?

Who are you?

It is fairly safe to assume that you are not a psychotherapist or
specialist social worker. It is possible that that you have not

had much formal training in counselling/interpersonal skills, other than that which is tailor-made to meet the specific aims of your organisation. It is unfortunately true that some people tend to list the things you are not and come up with the equation that volunteer equals amateur. In all but a small minority of cases this notion is to be strongly refuted.

You are someone with status and a role. You assume responsibilities and are given authority. The history of many voluntary organisations can be traced back to a person or group of people who recognised that there was an area of need in the community which was not being met by the statutory agencies. Through their activities and energies other people were motivated and the original recognition developed into a local or national organisation. Some of them, such as Barnardo's or the National Society for the Prevention of Cruelty to Children (NSPCC), have had a statutory role delegated to them and employ professionally qualified workers. However, most have stayed in the non-statutory sector. In order to maintain coherence and impetus as they grew, these organisations have stuck very closely to their original aims. This is how they are given their definition.

If you look at the annals of any voluntary organisation you will probably find they contain the records of mistakes and failures as well as successes. Over time, all these become absorbed into the experience of the group and become a hard-core of tried and tested knowledge. Thus, far from being amateur, such a group has a detailed and profound knowledge of a particular area of need. It has learnt how best to cope with the need and what are its own limitations.

You are a specialist

As a member of your organisation and representative of it to the world at large, and your clients in particular, you inherit that detailed and profound knowledge. Perhaps it takes you a little time to learn it and to feel confident. The same can be said of a social worker or psychotherapist. It is wrong to think of yourself as an amateur or to accept that judgement from other people. Rather, you are a specialist in your own area of concern. By the very fact that your organisation has continued to exist you have the evidence that your way of working is effective and as necessary as any professional field of work.

A volunteer's expertise may be threatening to a professional carer who has undergone a lengthy training. Further, when coming into contact with the professional world a volunteer may feel diminished by the other's confidence in her own training and abilities. The apparent exclusiveness which may exist among professionals can be threatening. But just as an articled clerk does not have to re-write the whole of English law in order to become a solicitor, you do not have to go through the whole of the development of your organisation to become a good and competent volunteer.

To continue the analogy further, there are areas of the law which need reform, areas which are outdated and areas which are distinctly quirky. So with your organisation, you may not know why things are done in a certain way or why you would not touch some problems with a 10-foot barge pole. You may be able to see areas where things could be done better. If you only joined your organisation last week or last year, you will feel distinctly inexperienced and perhaps out of your depth. But there are other volunteers and professionals who have the experience from which you can learn. They should be flexible enough to learn from your experience of looking at things with new eyes.

It is in the nature of all voluntary agencies that volunteers come and then they go again, but the agency carries on much the same. Provided you have the willingness to learn and grow in experience as a volunteer, you can count yourself as a specialist in your chosen work, with something positive to contribute. You have the expertise and experience of your organisation behind you. So long as you abide by guidelines and acknowledge your limitations, you are not an amateur, or in its perjorative sense, a do-gooder (what is wrong with doing good, anyway?).

You were born with ears

In terms of listening skills, no one can be trained to listen. What you can learn is how to listen in the way that will help your client the best. Such skills do not come with degrees and diplomas attached: they are what you have been practising to a varying extent all your life. A professional carer may know all there is about statutes, laws, benefits and so on. It does not mean that she will be any better (or worse) at sitting down with someone and letting him share what is on his mind.

Issues to think about

- What does your organisation do better than anyone else, voluntary or statutory?
- If your organisation did not exist, would the work be done as well by anyone else? Why/why not?

Who is the client?

To some extent you will already have defined your clients
before you ever became a volunteer. If you are interested in
pre-school nursery education you are unlikely to have joined
Help the Aged. Now you have become, or are hoping to
become, a volunteer in an organisation that devotes its
energies to a particular group of people. But is there a
difference between what you actually know about them and
what you think you know?

   We all carry inbuilt stereotypes around with us because they
are a way of coping with the world as we experience it:
policemen are helpful, nurses are wonderful, judges are
impartial. If we read about exceptions to these in the
newspaper they do not threaten our stereotypical picture,
rather they make it more firm and clear-cut – a patch of yellow
poppies in a field of red ones only serve to make the red ones
look redder. The above list, however, is of occupations, not
people. When we try to organise our fellow men and women
into nicely clear-cut stereotypes, the edges are blurred. Our
preconceived ideas can sometimes appear to be just that –
thoughts of how we would like people to be rather than how
they actually are. These can develop into a sort of common
currency between us that serve to give us all a sense of
security and invulnerability. Some examples are:

1 People who are depressed have only themselves to blame.
   They ought to pull themselves together, count their
   blessings and face up to life like the rest of us.
2 Nearly all women who are raped have only themselves to
   blame. Either they have led a man on or they have been
   alone in the street late at night. That is just asking for it.
3 Anyone who cannot pay their gas or electricity bills only
   have themselves to blame. They ought to be more careful in
   what they use and they ought to budget their money more
   wisely.

If we believe these three examples, it goes some way towards
reassuring ourselves that we can fend off mental distress by
our own efforts, we can be sure of our physical safety provided
we follow the rules, and we are good, upright citizens who
know where our responsibilities lie and will honour them.

   If you believe any of the above three examples it will take
more than can be written here to disabuse you of your beliefs.
However, to set the record straight:

1   Depression can happen to anyone at any time for any
number of reasons, or none at all. Not one of us is immune
from mental distress or illness. Some of the features of
depression are that a person cannot pull himself together,
that blessings become meaningless and that facing some
aspects of life are impossible.

2   A very large number of rapes take place in the victim's
home and by someone known to the victim. Any woman has
the right to say 'no' and the right to go where she will. To
believe otherwise is to blame the victim for the crime.

3   Households where there are young children, elderly
occupants or someone who is ill cannot economise on
heating bills beyond a certain level. It is impossible to
generalise on such an issue but circumstances change –
financial security cannot always be depended upon.

Don't jump to conclusions

Listening to your client with blinkered ears will not help him.
The only way you can know whether you are doing so is by
identifying the particular stereotypes you carry with you. If,
after listening to a client for five minutes, you mentally put
him in a box labelled 'irresponsible' or 'more money than
sense', you are automatically limiting your, and the client's,
options. How can you expect the client to be open with you if
you are metaphorically sticking labels on him, each with their
own set of preconceptions and expectations? There is a
difference between making use of information and experience
and jumping to prejudicial conclusions.

One way around this problem is to see a bit of yourself in
the client – 'there but for the grace of God . . .' This is not
meant to play upon the insecurities and fears which we all
have. So your client is in debt, depressed, not looking after
himself properly; if things in your own life had been a little bit
different, can you not see yourself in a similar predicament? It
may not be over-stating the case to say that it is *only* by seeing
a bit of yourself in the other person that you can care enough
to be able to help him.

Resisting temptation

If you go into voluntary work with the attitude 'these people
are not like me', then the temptation will be to try to make
them like you. Even given the status and access to other
peoples' lives that your voluntary work confers upon you,

what right have you to do that? A person has every right to
live in an untidy, grubby house if that is genuinely what he
wants to do. A person facing stress and pressure in his life has
every right to react by becoming depressed, if that can be said
to be a thing of choice. Again, if you can see something of
yourself in that person, you will gain an insight into why he
has chosen to live like that. You will reach an understanding of
what it feels like to be depressed because of outside
circumstances. If you see your client as totally 'other', you may
try to take over his home and make it a replica of your own,
regardless of his desires. You may make your client feel even
more guilty about his depression by forcing your own,
undepressed personality upon him.

Issues to think about

- Are your clients what you expect them to be? Give
  examples.
- How can you identify a stereotype?
- Are there any occasions when 'sticking a label' on a client is
  necessary?

What are you trying to do?

In two important ways it is impossible to provide a general
answer to this question.

First, the relationship that you build up with the client is
always defined by the specific aims of your organisation. It
would be nice to think that we are omnipotent, that when
presented with a client with a whole set of problems we can
roll up our sleeves, literally and metaphorically, and sort them
all out for him. Unfortunately, our powers are very limited; if
we tried to do all that we would probably finish by tying
ourselves and, even worse, the client in knots. You will have
many clients – to concentrate on one by doing things for him
that are outside your organisation's ambit may seem very
laudable. But it may lead to neglecting another client whose
needs your organisation is designed to meet. It may also take
you outside your sphere of competence.

What you can do is point the client in the direction of other
agencies and professionals who will take care of his other
needs. This overcomes one of the unhappiest aspects of the
voluntary sector, which is that each agency works in its own
way to answer particular needs. While there is not often
rivalry between different organisations, there is a palpable

absence of a sense of working together for the total care of the client. We become so taken up with the work of our own agency that we forget to look around and examine the possibilities of working more closely with other organisations. Perhaps the threat to our own agency's sense of identity and working practices is too great to be contemplated. When we are in danger of becoming possessive it is at an eventual cost to the client. Limiting information limits possibilities.

The second difficulty in defining what you are trying to do is that what goes on in any counselling relationship is unique to the two people involved. You do not always have to provide answers or give advice. Simply listening to your clients can be the most helpful and constructive thing to do. It may be all that the client wants or needs.

What can you aim for?

So, given that your role appears to be a passive one, what is there for you to aim for? One definition of any voluntary agency is that it is involved in problem-solving. The client comes to you, or is referred to you, because there is some difficulty that needs to be resolved. Therefore, you are trying to reach a resolution with the client. If you provide some definite end product, such as hot meals or medical equipment, then your aim is easy to define and its resolution will be both clear-cut and visible. But if you are working with people who are chronically ill or emotionally distressed, there is no clear-cut ending.

There is a tendency to think that it is acceptable to have aims that are not so clear-cut as, say, providing 60 hot meals a day. The danger of this approach has already been pointed out: to try to solve all your client's problems because you are not sure which particular ones are in your area of expertise is to invite catastrophe. It is important to the client, as well as yourself, that he knows what he can realistically expect your involvement to achieve. In order to do that you have to be clear in your own mind about your aims and limitations.

Drawing up a contract

Perhaps it will be appropriate to draw up a contract with your client. This need not be anything elaborate or even written down; it can be just a simple statement of what is available. It will, however, be a reference point that both of you can refer back to if necessary. It will say what can be expected as well as what you cannot provide. The contract should also state what you are both aiming for. If you cannot define this in the early stages, because you do not yet know the full extent of the client's situation, phrase it in general terms and come back to it at a later stage. Then you can be more specific. This would serve to give you both an idea of an end point and, by reviewing the contract, the client may be able to see for himself how far he has progressed. Perhaps, as your relationship develops, what he needs from you changes. To stop you both wandering about not quite knowing where you are, a definite reference point will show you where you have been and give pointers to where you ought to go.

Not taking control

It may be that your organisation has a practical side to it (i.e. providing equipment, physical help, money). However, so long as you are dealing with people and their emotional problems, it should *not* be your aim to sort out those problems *for* the client. Ultimately we are all in control of our own lives. That does not mean that we can always control what happens to us, whether those events originate from outside ourselves of whether they are within us. But our reactions to those events are our own, and what we need is help and understanding, not manipulation.

Therefore, what you are trying to do is help the client to be in control. You are trying to realise the aims which your organisation has set out to achieve and to recognise what is neither possible nor desirable for you to do. You need to know what you can expect from yourself and from your organisation, and you need to let the client know what he can expect from you.

Issues to think about

• If you were to draw up a contract with a client of yours, what would it include and what would it leave out?
• In what areas do you have a tendency to want to control your client (we all do)?
• How can you define a problem without 'sticking labels' on the client?

How do you do it?

You and your client have just met and are sitting down to start your time together. So what is, or should be, going through your mind and what is possibly going through his?

First impressions

If you have just met the client for the first time, you are probably making all sorts of judgements about him. Some of these you might not be consciously aware of. His physical appearance, clothing, accent and facial expression will all say something about him, and you will be busy trying to assess what that is. But he will also be doing the same thing with regard to you. If you give a misleading impression in those first few moments it may take quite some time to get over the hurdle you have created. There is not much you can do about your voice or basic physical appearance, though it would not hurt to listen to yourself and look at yourself in the mirror from time to time. But you can do something about your facial expression, which should be welcoming and open.

Let it show that you are there to be with the client and help him, rather than showing that you are anxious or nervous. If your client is unemployed, your wearing your own version of the crown jewels will create an immediate barrier between you. This can also apply to badges that express a particular belief or concern. So be aware of the impression that you might be giving to the client in those first few moments and try to make sure that it shows what it is of importance for him to know. You should not be putting on an act, but you should be keeping your anxieties to yourself and making the client feel as much at ease as is possible.

Your assessments of each other will continue, but after those initial moments your self-consciousness should diminish. The client has come because he has a problem, so the efforts of both of you should be directed towards this. What you reveal about yourself should be kept to a minimum because you are only relevant to his problem in your role as counsellor or befriender, not as a harrassed mother or an over-worked teacher.

Getting to know the client

Clients will differ in how well they can articulate their feelings and worries. It is easy to fall into the trap of thinking that someone who can talk freely and with apparent ease is easier to work with than someone who has great difficulty in this area. Certainly you want your client to tell you something about himself, his situation and the problems that he has at the moment. But telling you in too many words can be as difficult for you as telling you in too few.

Do not rush your client. It is likely that he will be nervous when he first meets you, especially if he is not used to talking about himself and his problems. He may have a tendency either to talk at great length about something that is not relevant or is only incidental to the problem that has brought him to you. Or he may not be able to think of a way to start off and continue to sit in miserable silence. In either case you will need to put the client at ease, either by allowing him to talk on for a little while until you begin to see him relax, or by showing that silence does not bother you. In those initial moments take your pace from the client because to do otherwise is to put another pressure on him when he already feels himself to be in a stressful situation.

You need to be aware of focusing on the first problems you are offered by the client. It is much easier for a client to talk about how he is having problems with the car than it is to talk about how frightened he is at the thought of being made redundant. Sometimes it is a matter of just sitting and listening until the client feels confident enough to get himself off the peripheral subject and on to talking about what is really bothering him. Other people may plant 'clues' in what they are saying so that, with a little discernment on your part, you can ask the questions that will lead him into talking about the main problem. Yet another person may have such difficulty in expressing himself that he may want you to do it for him. This can be in the form of questions or statements in answer to which he will give very short replies or just a nod or shake of the head. If you are forced into asking questions, try to make sure that they require a fuller answer than just 'yes' or 'no'.

However well or badly the client expresses himself is not a reflection on the depth of emotion that he is feeling. It may be that he is trying to put that emotion into words for the first time, or that this is one of the few times when he has let himself feel the true depth of the pain. Either way, he is going to be making himself work very hard and you should be giving him all the help that you can. This can be in the form of questions (not interrogation) or repeating to him something that he has just said with the aim of leading him into an elaboration of the comment. You may re-state the gist of the last few comments so that he knows that you have understood and he can further clarify any misunderstanding. What should never happen is that you do most of the talking; keep your comments and questions to a minimum.

Silences

The art of 'being with' the client when he is not actually saying anything is a difficult one to cultivate. If he is trying to express very deep and painful emotions, it may take him some time to sort them out and identify them in such a way that he can put words to them. This means that there may be quite long spells of silence. You need to be able to identify the times when there is silence because the client needs some prompting from you and silence because he is struggling with his feelings. It is inevitable that you will sometimes get the two confused, but experience will help. Never be frightened of the silence or view it as something that should not happen. It can be that it is because of the secure and caring atmosphere you have created for the client that he feels able to explore the depth of his emotions instead of denying them, even to himself.

The effects on you

What the client is saying will have its effect on you, especially if he is telling you of very strong or painful emotions. If you are mentally composing your shopping list or wondering how quickly you can bring this meeting to an end while he is telling you how suicidal he feels, there is very little point in your being there at all. The alternative is that you share some of his feelings, that you be with him in his despair or anxiety and that together you work out a way forward. Neither this book nor any other can tell you how to do this, for it is something that can only be worked out through experience. But if you do find yourself planning your next trip to the supermarket, or you come out of an hour's session with a very depressed client feeling wonderful, you can be sure that you are doing it wrong.

   Although we shall discuss how to look after yourself later in the book, it is appropriate to say here that you must be sure that there is someone within your organisation to whom you can talk about how you are feeling. If you know that there is such a person to whom you can turn after you have been with a difficult client, you are less likely to remain aloof from him, defending yourself while you are with him.

The end of the session

Bringing your time together to a close can be a problem. Sometimes the client will decide for himself, sometimes you will feel that you have both achieved all that is possible for the time being. If your client has been through a difficult and painful time you should ensure that he is feeling able to face the world again. Telling someone who is crying that his time is up will not help either him or your future relationship, even if it is convenient for you at the time. If you are going to see him again, make sure that he knows when and where, or at least that you will be in touch in the near future. If your organisation is such that he is free to get in touch with someone at any time, reassure him of this. Once he has gone, or you have left, assess how you are feeling. If you know that the interview has left feelings in you that need to be dealt with, do it. Talk to someone else within your organisation, in confidence, and share your own feelings – they are as important as those of the client.

Issues to think about

• What are the assessments that you make of someone simply by his appearance?
• What are the best ways of encouraging someone to share his feelings?
• Who in your organisation can you can talk to about how *you* feel?

Summing up

How you feel about yourself and how you feel about your client make a difference to the quality of the care that you can give both to him and to yourself. The client needs to know who you are, why you are there and what he can expect from you. You need to know why you are there, what it is reasonable for your client to expect of you and how best you can give it. One of the most vital things you can do for your client, if not the most vital, is to listen to him, to give him care, security and time in which to express his feelings and concerns.

The rest of this book will assume that you have, or are willing to learn, the skills by which you can do this. It is only from the basis of being willing to listen to your client that you can hope to help him in any other way.

3 Emotions, feelings and frames of mind

Being in control

The purpose and effect of offering a client emotional support is:
- to encourage him to express what he is feeling, thereby
- helping reduce his sense of isolation,
- helping reduce his fear and anxiety, and
- helping restore his confidence and self-esteem

By doing these things the aim, ultimately, is to help him regain his sense of control over his own life and therefore over his own happiness. This may seem rather a tall order. It raises the question of how listening is supposed to be able to do all that. In the long run, ought not the volunteer rather devote her energies to offering some practical assistance which might improve the day-to-day circumstances in which the client is having to live? On some rare and exceptional occasions this may be so. But the link between how a person feels about himself on an emotional level and the outward circumstances of his life is not always simple.

What follows in this chapter is one explanation of how our feelings fit in with other aspects of our lives and why, therefore, it is very important to understand them. We point out how feelings and states of mind can be hard to identify and explain. This can result in confusion and a sense of vulnerability. If we are confused we do not know what to believe or what to expect. This makes us vulnerable and insecure, and so we do not know what to do. By helping someone understand his own feelings, we can help him recognise what he wants and is able to do. If he is more aware of this, then he can be more in control of achieving what he wants.

We offer a small amount of information on a particular psychological state which may beset many of the clients with whom you may become involved: post-traumatic stress disorder. By helping you recognise some standard responses to traumatic situations, we hope to put you in a position to help your clients better. The chapter ends with some thoughts on where your feelings fit in. To begin with we will take a look at 'inner' and 'outer' lives.

Feeling and doing

So far we have made the distinction between emotional and practical support without making it very clear what we take these to mean. Perhaps we should not need to explain what we think the differences are. After all, everyone can distinguish between arranging for the plumber to call and listening while someone describes how afraid he is. It is not that difficult to tell whether what is under discussion is the smelly drain or somebody's feelings. Or is it? We need to know about how the two might be connected, and how that affects the way you, as a volunteer, need to look at the situation.

Recognising emotions

Although we talk about feelings and actions in different ways, we often need to explain each in terms of the other. For that reason it is worth exploring the connection a little more closely. Emotions such as fear, anger and joy 'move us' to act in certain ways. When we are afraid, we often want to run away or freeze to the spot or do something that amounts to the same sort of thing. We normally think about taking steps to protect ourselves, though in some circumstances we have special reasons for not doing so if there is something more important to us than our personal safety. The other side of this is that when we watch the way someone else behaves and listen to what he says, we can usually tell whether or not he is afraid.

Similarly, feeling angry makes us want to lash out, either with our arms and legs or with our tongues. We want to hurt someone or something. This is what anger is about. Often we do not actually do it, but we may well clench our fists or our teeth. As with fear, we often recognise how it feels inside when we are angry, and we also recognise when other people are angry from the way they behave and the way they seem to be feeling.

With a little thought you can readily map the sorts of feelings and sensations associated with other emotions and, on each occasion, you will also, probably, have some idea of the sorts of things that arouse those emotions. That is, you recognise the objects of them. When we are angry we are angry *with someone or about something*. When we are jealous or ashamed we feel that there is, there must be, something which explains these emotions.

In fact, we sometimes need to be clear about what the object of our emotions is before we can put a name to what we are feeling at all. Think, for instance, of those times when you know a situation churns you up. You know that there is a lot going on inside you but it is hard to sort out what it is. Often you need to discover this before you can explain it. Is it anger with your boss, himiliation at a reprimand, shame at your own behaviour, perhaps all? To be clear you have to know the focus of your strong feelings.

Sometimes we have no difficulty looking at what it is that is making us feel the way we do. On other occasions we are less willing or able to do so. Think about jealousy for a moment. How many people recognise, or are prepared to admit, that their behaviour on a particular occasion is motivated by jealousy? It may be very obvious to everyone else that you are jealous – but not to you.

Issues to think about

- Are there any emotions which you have never felt?
- Do you suspect that there may be any you have not allowed yourself to become aware of feeling? What are they?
- Are there any emotions which you might think it particularly hard to recognise in other people?
- Are there any feelings or emotions in yourself or others which you find it particularly hard to accept or to deal with?

Moods and states of mind

Emotions, sometimes with their characteristic physical accompaniments, and with their tendency to make us want to behave in a certain sort of way, are not the only feelings which you will work with as a volunteer, though. Most of us are also subject to other states of mind which are reflected in our behaviour. By a state of mind we mean not something which explains why we behave in a certain way in particular circumstances, but something which colours the way we look at the world and the whole way we react to it.

Depression, anxiety and despair all fall into this group. The point is that we do not think about this group of feelings in the same way that we think about our emotions, and we do not expect to recognise them, or understand them, or respond to them in the same sort of way. Sometimes depression and anxiety are linked to a particular set of circumstances, but on other occasions this may not be the case. There may not be anything, here and now, in general or in particular, that is making us depressed.

There is no definite sort of behaviour that allows us to spot, straight away and on every occasion, when someone else is depressed. Some people over-eat or buy new clothes; others drink; others sleep. To take another example, in the case of anxiety, it may make us work extra hard or it may get in the way of our working altogether.

Clearly, the situation is more complicated than at first it seemed. If you add to this other sorts of feelings – nervousness or panic for instance, the picture becomes one where it is far from clear where to draw the line between what people are doing and what they are feeling. There is clearly some connection between what they are feeling and what they do, but this may be both complicated and confusing for both them and others.

Issues to think about

- Do you always recognise, at the time, when you are depressed or anxious? If so, how?
- Have you ever managed to persuade yourself out of a state of mind that you do not want to be in? If so, how?
- Are there any people who seem to have a particular way of expressing their feelings who you find particularly easy, or difficult, to get on with? What are those ways?
- Do these people remind you of others in your life? Who? In what way?

Expressing feelings

Since there are many complicating factors, the line between practical and emotional support begins to get rather blurred. It is not that we cannot tell the difference between sending for the plumber and offering support to someone who is depressed. Of course we can, but the point is that we may be doing both, or one rather better than the other.

The second important thing to bear in mind is that if someone is not completely sure how he feels, then this may well affect decisions about what he can, or wants to do. Practical tasks remain undone not always because your client does not have the money, skill or information. Often your client is not doing something because his frame of mind makes other things more noticeable or more important. The mental effort involved in getting the practical task done is too great.

This is why it is important to discover, and to let people discover for themselves, what they are feeling. The most usual and effective way of doing this is by encouraging them to talk about the way they see situations. Often the very process of putting what we feel into words helps us to become more clear about what is going on inside us. What is going on inside us has implications for what goes on outside, that is, for the practical details of our lives.

For instance, we have suggested that feeling angry and feeling afraid are both emotions which make us behave in a certain way because of how we feel about something. But it is not always clear what that something is. A client whose wife is in hospital may well be able to say that he feels very afraid but unable to explain to himself, or to you, what exactly he is afraid of. He may be afraid of losing her; of not being able to cope with her pain; of not being able to support and care for their children; or of having to give up his work and social life to accept new and un-asked-for responsibilities. Perhaps all of these. Or perhaps he finds the uncertainty of the whole situation the thing that frightens him most. The point is that if he cannot sort out what he is afraid of, then he does not know what to do to overcome his fears, in so far as this may be possible.

Understanding and control

This gets to the nub of what listening, in the sense we are talking about it, is about. When a client expresses his feelings to someone else, then he struggles to make them comprehensible. He talks about what his feelings make him want to do, or not to do, and about how the way he sees the world makes him feel. As he expresses these things in a way other people might understand, he may well come to understand them better himself. When he understands things better he will be in a position to exercise more control over his future happiness.

If we do not know and cannot explain what is going on inside us and how we feel, then we are confused. This makes it very hard for us to decide what we need to do to make ourselves feel better and more in control of our lives. When our emotions are in turmoil, and when we cannot understand or explain our feelings, then we tend to feel helpless, vulnerable, and as if anything we do is probably pointless and irrelevant.

As a listener, it is your job to be able to sort out, in you own mind, the difference, for instance, between being afraid of something or being anxious; between being depressed or lacking in confidence. If the problem you are presented with seems to be a purely practical one – the drain is leaking – ask yourself why your client has not sorted this out. There may be a practical reason why he has tried and been unable to have it mended, or it may be something to do with his frame of mind that has made him feel that it is beyond him to try.

Issues to think about

- In what circumstances might performing a practical task or making a practical arrangement increase your client's sense of being in control of his life, and in what circumstances do you run the risk of making him feel even more hopeless and helpless than he did before?
- Give an example from your own life.
- Give an example of a family member or friend.

Post-traumatic stress disorder

In the course of your work, if you listen well, you will meet with more ways of feeling, and more expressions of them, than you would have thought imaginable. But there are also certain groups of physical and emotional responses which you may come to recognise with some frequency. In particular, these will be the responses, either immediate or delayed, to traumatic situations.

When people are part of some situation or event which is life-threatening (either to themselves or to someone they are close to), or which is likely to seriously alter life as they know it, this will probably lead to some extremely strong physical and psychological reactions. Sometimes these reactions happen straight away, sometimes they are delayed for weeks, months or years. Some people experience many of a cluster of physical and psychological symptoms, others relatively few. Perhaps you may be familiar with one famous instance of this particular response, which was identified as affecting many thousands of otherwise strong and healthy people: it was first described as shell shock.

For the past 70 years there has been a growing appreciation of, and increasing information about, what is now sometimes referred to as post-traumatic stress. More is known about the sorts of situations which give rise to this state, and there is more awareness and acknowledgement that each of us, as an individual or as a member of a group, is likely to experience post-traumatic stress to some degree at some time in our lives.

It is not just the horror of first-hand experience of military combat which creates this type of shock in us. Any serious threat to ourselves or people close to us may result in post-traumatic stress. Rape, sudden destruction of our home or community, or contact with those who have recently experienced violence or a major accident can all affect us in this way.

What are the effects?

Normally you may expect someone who has experienced an event which is traumatic to be aware of at least two of the following:

- recurrent, distressing recollections, which intrude on other things they are thinking about
- recurrent dreams and nightmares
- sensations of reliving the experience, with flashbacks and hallucinations associated with the event
- extreme distress in circumstances which resemble the traumatic one or which provide forceful reminders (such as anniversaries)

As well as this you may expect several of the following:

- efforts to avoid thoughts and feelings connected with the event
- efforts to avoid activities which arouse memories
- difficulty in remembering important parts of the traumatic event
- a noticeable loss of interest in current activities
- feelings of detachment and estrangement
- difficulty in feeling or expressing affection
- the sense of a diminished and unsatisfying future in life

This list descibes some of the ways a person may find their awareness limited. We would think of someone as suffering from post-traumatic stress if he noticed at least three of them to any degree. As well as these it is likely that there will be respects in which your client, if that is what he is, will be *more* aware or sensitive. In a state of post-traumatic stress he is likely to be aware of at least two of the following:

- difficulty in staying or falling asleep
- irritability and outbursts of anger
- difficulty concentrating
- extreme watchfulness (for example, making sure he sits with his back to the wall)
- a tendency to be extremely jumpy in response to relatively small sounds or movements (officially called 'exaggerated startle response')
- a tendency to have marked physical reactions – breaking out in a sweat or being sick – in circumstances strongly associated with the trauma

Most of us have experienced some of these things at some time: we know that in time most of them fade or pass. The point here is that if someone is showing signs of feeling large clusters of these feelings and states all at the same time he may need more help than you can offer to overcome the distress they will be causing him.

So how can you help?

Faced with such aweful distress you may well wonder where, or how, you can possibly start to help. Indeed, if the trauma has been extreme and the symptoms acute your client may, for a time at least, need medical help. But traumatic situations are not altogether different from the ones we considered earlier, so the suggestions on pages 26–30 may help here, too. Your client may be wrestling with a number of conflicting emotions instead of just one or two, and his feelings may swing violently between extremes, but he may still find the same sorts of opportunities and considerations appropriate:

- He may want to talk to get his own ideas, however contradictory they may seem, clear in his head and *out of his head* into the world (i.e., you).
- He may need reassuring that it is all right to have all these feelings at once – that he is not going mad.

- He may take some comfort from knowing that he is not the only person who has felt the way he does. It is not his own personal weakness. Other people in traumatic circumstances have reacted in the same sorts of ways that he is doing. His *reactions* are normal, therefore he is normal.
- He may be encouraged to know that there can be an end to his current terrifying and miserable state and that, in time, he will be able to look forward to a future over which he will, once again, be able to have at least some control.

As a volunteer you cannot begin by informing him of all these things; but if you yourself understand that they can be true, you can listen in the right way, ask the right questions and so lead him to understand for himself.

Issues to think about

- Looking back on it, when have you experienced these responses to a traumatic experience?
- Are you clear what effects giving your undivided attention to someone else's distress may have on you? What are they?
- Are you aware of any emotions, feelings or memories which you are not prepared to have rekindled in you? What are they?

Your own feelings

These questions lead naturally to the last area to be considered in this chapter. What is the nature of the contract, the understanding, between you and your client and where does that leave you? You may find yourself in a relationship in which your client reveals intimate feelings about extremely personal aspects of his life. These in turn may evoke extremely strong feelings in you. But he is not your friend. The relationship exists purely for his benefit and to meet his needs. It is not reciprocal. You need to think how you are going to perform the balancing act of meeting your client's needs while protecting and preserving yourself. In chapter 2 we considered how you must not be defensive towards your client. The way to do this is to be aware of how your feelings might be affected and who you can talk to for your benefit.

We shall talk more about looking after yourself in chapter 8; here we shall concentrate on two specific areas. Both arise from the limitations of your relationship with your client in emotional terms. The first concerns the dangers and difficulties of caring too much. The second concerns the way your relationship with your client can change over time if your job is to act as a long-term befriender.

Caring can be hard

Given that you and your client meet for the purpose of helping him, and given your meetings are likely to involve the expression of strong emotions, you need to be clear how you are going to allow your own feelings to be involved. Obviously you are not going to sit like a pudding, giving off strong messages to the effect that none of this has anything to do with you. But at the same time it is the case that the problems, feelings and pains which emerge are his and not yours.

Making it clear that you understand and appreciate how someone feels is different from saying that you are feeling the same way that he does, here and now. It may be that his feelings rekindle similar ones in you. If so, that is your problem. It is one you will need to sort out with the appropriate member of your organisation or in your personal relationships.

But it may not be that his sadness reminds you of sadnesses of your own. Because of the situation you may feel sad with and for him. You may, indeed, feel very sorry for him and experience a great deal of anger and helplessness because of your inability to see the possibility of any change in his situation. From time to time you will meet situations where your overriding feeling is simply that 'things like this ought not to happen'. There is something in all of us that makes us unwilling to accept the misery that results from cruelty, ignorance or just plain misfortune. Other people's suffering can be hard to bear. You will need to work out for yourself how you cope best with the fact that, from time to time, however hard we try, bad things happen.

Issues to think about

- Can you have fun or give yourself a treat after spending time with a client facing insoluble problems and overwhelming misery? How?

Long-term relationships

Finally, think for a minute about how contact with a client over a long period of time is likely to affect you. In what we have talked about so far we have tended to think about the situation on a single occasion or during a fairly short period of crisis. But not all befriending, of course, is of that sort. Sometimes you may be in contact with a family for years, and that calls for a special sort of awareness.

In some sense you may become part of that family, and consideration of them may become part of your habitual routine. You may get to know them very well, and they you. The questions then become: what are you doing in the situation? Are your reasons for staying involved the same as your reasons for becoming involved in the first place? Could you remove yourself from the situation in a way which would not be personally hurtful to family members? Could another volunteer take over from you and provide your clients with the same service?

The difficulty, of course, is that as you and your clients get to know each other well, more of your own individual and idiosyncratic personality becomes involved and the relationship can become more akin to a friendship. You may become accepted for who you are rather than for the service you provide. You need to make sure that the service is still delivered.

Dependency: yours or your clients'?

This very process of providing a service over a long period of time can create problems of its own too. The major one is that there is a risk of your clients becoming dependent on you. We all tend to take things for granted when they are a regular part of our lives. By making sure that you provide consistent, dependable support or help you may encourage a state of affairs where your clients find it increasingly more difficult, rather than less so, to cope without you. We have talked about the needs of your clients. It is important for you to be aware of fostering even greater need by encouraging them to rely on you to provide what they otherwise might learn to provide themselves.

This is another of the balancing acts you will have to learn to perform: another judgement you will have to make that it is hard to offer guidelines to cover. On one hand, in the initial stages your client needs to develop confidence in you; on the other, he must not lose confidence in his own abilities. He needs to know that he can rely on you to be there to help him do some of the things he needs to do, but he also needs to discover, in time, that he can do these things for himself, even if you are not there.

Parting can be difficult, too

When the job is done and the client no longer needs your services, you have to find a way of bringing your contact to an end. Sometimes there may be a natural break to indicate when the time has come, but this is not always the case. On other occasions you may have agreed at the beginning to a fixed period of, say, six months or a year. In that case you can prepare for your farewells as you approach the agreed date. But usually it is not as clear-cut as this. In the first place there may be some difficulty, for both you and your client, in deciding when there is no more useful purpose behind your relationship. Secondly, you both may be reluctant to withdraw from the contact.

At this point it may be necessary for you to discuss the differences between you as a friend and you as a befriender. Perhaps you will want to think about future contact on a friendly basis if that is appropriate, while gradually loosening your ties as the representative of your organisation. Whatever your decisions about future contact, your separation from the clients you know well in your counselling role needs to be prepared for and given the appropriate time and consideration. Separations are rarely easy, but some can be handled better than others.

We suggest that it might be helpful to consider with your clients what you achieved together. Look at the good parts, but acknowledge the bad and difficult ones, too. It is tempting to skate over the parts that did not go so well, but when you say your farewells it is easier to separate if you do not leave things that are important to you unsaid.

Issues to think about

- How do you assess the value of your involvement with a client over a prolonged period of time?
- When does a client/volunteer relationship turn into a friendship? Can you have both at the same time?
- How can you tell if the client is becoming dependent on you?
- How can you tell if you are becoming dependent on the client?

Finally, it may help to look to the future. Acknowledge that, in your counselling role, you will be moving on to offer similar help to other people, acknowledge what you have gained from your time together, and discuss with your client what he will be going on to achieve. The difficulties of separation, while still there, can be kept in perspective by being placed in their context between the job that has been done and your separate plans for the future.

4 Other relationships

Families, friends and acquaintances

Very few people who contact voluntary agencies such as
Relate, or statutory ones such as the Probation Service, are
actually alone in the world when they refer themselves to the
agency. They are not *just* clients. They are probably members
of families and they may also be employers, neighbours,
churchgoers, flatmates, friends or pub goers. There are, on the
face of it, plenty of other people your clients could talk to, and
they probably do.

Their contacts may provide them with material support and
comfort, a sense of security, emotional and moral support and
very often intellectual challenge and stimulation. Ideally,
family life, for example, may fulfil a variety of needs for each
of the members, whatever their role in that family. But it may
also create pressures and problems. There may be some sense
of understanding, someone to talk to, someone to listen,
someone to acknowledge feelings and to respond to them, or
there may be none of these. For some clients it may be the
relationships within the family which create the difficulties.

Perhaps, more importantly, most people have friends. The
significance of this is that, unlike families, friends are chosen.
These are often the tailor-made relationships. Friends
sometimes choose each other because they agree on many
important matters, and sometimes they choose each other
because they are so different that they meet some special need
in each other. In either case friends are the people who usually
know most about each other and who answer many, if not
most, of each other's needs.

Meanwhile, neighbours may simply maintain a nodding acquaintanceship or casual familiarity. They acknowledge each other, perhaps daily, without ever getting to know each other better. Or, in the corner shop, they may listen to, or share, the same information and gossip, being part of a different sort of group, with some views and attitudes in common. When they get to work, or evening classes, or the club, they will be with others who, in a variety of ways, may share their interests, aims and problems. People grumble on buses, tell jokes at work, drop in for a pint, ring each other up, eat together, visit and watch the same TV.

As well as all these there may be the socially unacceptable and illicit relationships which create conflict and tend to be hidden. These are the friendships which offend against social, religious, sexual or racial conventions or loyalties, and which are likely to create difficulties for the individual. There are people whose importance to use we can and do publicise. There are others whose significance to us it may be very difficult to acknowledge publicly.

Social isolation

Before looking at the other relationships your client may have, perhaps it is important to mention another group of clients. Some people may refer themselves to your organisation precisely because they feel the need for some relationship. Increasing social isolation, in part due to unemployment and exemplified by 'bedsit lands', means that an increasing number of people find themselves without lasting or significant relationships.

With no work to go to and no one to come home to, relationships are not easily established. Lack of money makes it difficult to take part in activities which might lead to friendships. The result is that for many there may be a sense of physical and emotional isolation. You may find yourself with clients whose major need is to make some meaningful contact with another person.

This group may also include people who, for physical or emotional reasons, find it hard to make or maintain significant contacts. Such people are trapped between the need for such relationships and the inability to initiate them. Here, your major task may be to help your client to involve himself with other people.

Issues to think about

- Who else is your client connected to? How many people? Who and where are they?
- Who provides for his material, emotional, social and intellectual needs?

So why you, and why now?

Since there seem to be so many other people most of your clients could talk to, it clearly raises the questions why you, and why now? How, in other words, do you fit into your client's scheme of things, and how should you? The following ideas may help provide the answers to some of these questions.

People are likely to need someone new or different to talk to if

- they are changing
- their relationships are changing
- their situation or circumstances are changing

This is because these changes may well give rise to new needs or problems for which your client's existing networks do not, for the time being at least, provide satisfactory answers.

Changes

Before going on to look at how you and your client look at the other people he is involved with it would perhaps be useful to stop and think a little about different sorts of change and how we react to them. Sometimes we feel 'a change is as good as a rest'; sometimes it is not. Sometimes, instead of being refreshing and stimulating, new situations pose a risk and seem rather threatening. 'Better the devil you know' after all 'than the devil you don't'.

So when are changes good and when are they not so good? The answer to this has something to do with what is changing and also something to do with the way we react. It is usually a combination of the two. Some situations help us get more out of life; some create stress and pressure. What is it about us that allows us to grow through some crises and feel totally beaten and deflated in others?

Changes we expect

Let us look first at the sort of changes we go through just in
the normal run of events. In terms of our personal
development, we change from being children to being adults.
Some of us become parents, many adjust to middle and old age.
While this is happening we find ourselves adapting to different
roles which may carry different status. We begin school, start
work, leave home, get married, secure promotions with their
changing responsibilities, launch children on their own
independent lives, lose jobs, retire and often move house to fit
in with these other changes.

Unexpected and unplanned changes

As if this were not enough, we have to cope with unexpected
and unplanned changes, too. Deaths, desertions, disablements,
losses and sometimes unwanted dependencies fall into this
group. In addition to these essentially 'personal' changes the
list gets longer if we add the community changes which may
touch all of us at various points. Natural disasters such as
hurricanes and landslides are only two of the long list of
events which can change the course of life for large groups of
people. Others include war, economic upheavals and major
disasters such as plane crashes or fires.

In view of all this it would seem reasonable to expect people
to be used to change and able to handle it. But the fact is that
some people seem to cope with all changes better than others
do, and all of us are better at coping in some sorts of situations
than we are in others. If, as a volunteer, you are hoping to
assist people who are seeking help in coping with new
situations, then it may help to have thought a little about some
of the ways people respond to different sorts of change.

Crises call for new solutions

In this discussion 'a change' is more than leaving home to take
the sea air for a week (though leaving the cat and the garden
can prove stressful for some). The sort of change here is one
which someone sees as an upset in the normal, usual, steady
state of things and one which is at least a little worrying and at
worst anxiety-producing. In fact, potentially it is a crisis.
Looking back at the list of changes mentioned before, the point
to notice is that for most of us, most of the time, those
changes present us with new difficulties for which we have to
find new solutions. We cannot set out to learn in advance how

to be a successful adolescent or practice losing our job or a parent or a friend. These events present us with a crisis, and we may have to learn to cope as we go along, especially if we have not met similar crises in the past.

A threat, a loss or a challenge

Different people, though, seem to react rather differently. Some people see crises as threats, others as losses. For others, they are challenges. How people see these new experiences makes a difference to how they cope and how they can best be helped. If something happens which makes us feel out of control, we feel threatened and anxious. (We have already considered reducing fear and anxiety in chapter 3.) If what happens leaves us with an overwhelming sense of loss, then we will probably respond with mourning, and in some cases, depression. The client who is coping with loss will need help expressing this, coming to terms with the pain of it and coping with the various tasks necessary to overcome the loss to the extent to which this is possible.

The next, and perhaps most hard-to-describe way we may respond to a crisis is to regard it as a challenge. Sometimes a change is easy to see as a challenge – a new job, retirement, a new member of the family. Sometimes it is much harder to see the change as one which will provide us with the opportunity to enhance the quality of our lives. But the fact is that even the most devastating of losses and the most cruel disappointments can inspire some people with the energy and determination to find new solutions to their problems, and so increase their sense of control over their own lives and the quality of their existence.

New situations, new needs

Whatever the change and however much of a crisis it presents for your client, he is likely to need support. He will need it not only from you, a new and different person, attuned to his new and different needs, but from his well-established networks of contacts, too. That is if he still has them. But it seems that, when a crisis hits, at least to begin with, not all the old friends will necessarily be of most help, even it they are available.

In fact, long-standing relationships may be the very ones which find it hardest to adapt to new situations and new needs. Old friends and close family expect people to stay largely the same. At least part of the sense of security which

goes with these 'comfortable' relationships comes from the fact
that they are habitual. People rely on their friends, often,
precisely because they do stay the same. Major changes rock
the boat. For this reason there may well be pressure on your
client from various quarters not to change. When couples
separate, each may receive very little support from their oldest
mutual friends who may not want to cope with the change.

Having thought a little about change in general, it is time to
consider those specific situations when changes affecting your
client may result in his needing you.

When clients change

Take a situation when the change your client is facing is one
which affects primarily him. Even in such a case, because we
are involved with other people, a change in ourselves may also
necessitate a change in our lifestyle.

A client may find himself facing depression or a drink
problem. His current friends, relatives and acquaintances may
not be willing or able to help. They may not expect, or be
prepared to accept this change in him, and he may not want to
ask anything different or new of them. Dealing with a drink
problem may commit your client to abandoning precisely those
contacts he saw himself deriving strength from previously –
his drinking companions. Even if drinking was not seen as the
sole or even the major reason for those contacts, it may well be
an aspect of the situation which others are not prepared to
change. A game of golf, an evening of darts, a meal out may
inevitably mean drinking for your client; for others it may play
an insignificant part which they see no reason to alter. Your
client may need to avoid these contacts, at least for a while.
Your job may to help him through the transition.

When relationships change

On the other hand, it may well be that some important
relationship has changed for the client and that this is why he
is in contact with you. Death and marital breakdown are
obvious examples, though by no means the most frequent.
Children grow up and leave home, accidents happen,
friendships shift, interests change and babies are born. All of
these may have consequences in terms of relationships. The
death of a friend is a loss which will inevitably lead to grief. It
may also serve to confront your client with his own mortality
in exactly the circumstances in which the person with whom

he might have discussed this is no longer there. It is not always possible to prepare for death beforehand, and afterwards, the opportunity is no longer there.

Similarly, marital breakdown may lead to a variety of responses, from feelings of liberation to a sense of complete and total devastation. Some feelings seem to be shared by many people who experience divorce, others are less frequent. Your client may now miss a sympathetic ear, or someone to care for. He may, above everything else, need to practice being himself rather than half a couple. In circumstances like these you may be called upon, through your agency, to provide support during a time when many adjustments have to take place.

For the client, the old relationships and alliances have vanished or broken down. He may need to re-group in 'neutral territory' before re-entering his own changed world. If his marriage had been long-standing, then it is likely that all or most of his important relationships will be affected by its dissolution. Neither his family nor his wife's may want to be involved (they will have their own adjustments to make), and their mutual friends may be even more difficult to approach.

When circumstances change

To take the third example of the client for whom circumstances have changed, the volunteer may find herself confronted by someone wrestling with redundancy, or clearing up after a burglary. Suddenly circumstances are different. The ex-foreman does not now have the same reason to get out of bed in the morning. He does not view himself or his world as he used to and he assumes, probably rightly, that many other people view him differently, too.

He has things to sort out and, at least to start with, his dependent family and his ex-colleagues may not be the most helpful people to turn to. In so far as his role has changed, his relationships may change, too. He will need to discover how much of himself was tied up in his job and his role. He may discover, too, how much of the way he related to other people, and they to him, depended on that role which has changed. He may look for a new contact – you – to help him explore, experiment and discover the new 'him'.

To summarise, the client who uses the volunteer may want to talk about things he cannot talk about with others, or in a way in which he is not used to talking with others. This may be because he has changed, or they have, or the situation has.

Issues to think about

- What has changed for your client which makes him come to someone like you, now?
- What other relationships does he have which might be useful to him now?
- What does he need from you now? How do you know?
- For how long is he likely to need these things?
- Are you the person in the best position to offer what your client needs?

Your place in your client's life

Looked at in this way, it is plain that your client may want to use his relationship with you in one or more of a variety of ways. Here are a few of the possibilities which have already been introduced in Chapters 2 and 3. Apart from those occasions on which he is seeking information, advice, practical assistance or resources, a client may wish to:

- benefit from relating in a particular way not allowed him by his other contacts
- practice new ways of relating
- discover his feelings by giving vent to them
- simply unburden himself by expressing strong feelings
- work out his thoughts by giving voice to new, difficult, dangerous or frightening ideas
- develop the capacity to relate

In all of these cases he is likely to feel that he is getting some moral support from you, and this may well 'rub off' on the other aspects of his life. Suppose that, as a probation volunteer, the change you identify in an adolescent youth is simply that he is growing up fast. Your answer to 'what does he want, now?' is that he wants befriending. He wants relationships with an adult who will treat him as an equal, not as a mother, teacher, employer, or pack leader might, but as a friend and ally. If you can give him that he will be able to practice being an adult in a way which might be quite difficult for him in the company of either his immature friends or of his parents.

Or suppose that as a Victim Support volunteer you decide that your client, who has survived a violent attack, needs the opportunity to express his anger, fear, shame and sense of helplessness without any risk that this expression will 'spill over' into the rest of his life. He is confiding in you something which he may not intend to share with anyone else. Initially, he simply wants an outlet for his feelings, though he may subsequently find that he has a mirror or a sounding board for them. As a result of expressing his feelings, he may understand them better and find that they have changed.

As a volunteer, reading this you will be able to supply your own examples of the wide variety of ways that your clients make use of their contact with you. Your examples, like the ones sketched above, will probably indicate that something about your client may well change as a result of his contact with you and that these changes may well affect the rest of his relationships.

Issues to think about

- How might your client's life change because of his contact with you?
- How are the changes going to affect his other relationships?

These questions lead on to another one which we consider below.

Should you become involved in your clients' other relationships?

From what has been said so far, the answer would seem to be that it is impossible not to be involved. But there is a difference between knowing that your contact may affect your client's behaviour in other aspects of his life and actively involving yourself with third persons. If we understand the question to be whether you should try to get involved with other people who are close to your client, then it is impossible to answer before looking at some other closely interwoven questions. These are:

- Which other relationships?
- At whose request?
- To what end?
- For how long?

Who decides?

If you are befriending a delinquent adolescent, do you also maintain contact with his parents? If you work for Age Concern or Cancercare, do you assume contact with any neighbours, children or close friends? The answer must surely be – it depends. It depends on the views of at least three different people on at least three different considerations.

The three people initially involved are first the client, second the volunteer and third the other person or people in question. On some occasions the agency represented by the volunteer may also have some say in the matter since levels of contact may be an agency or professional decision.

Presuming the client is a responsible adult who has entered into the arrangement with the volunteer of his own free will, then he, of course, has an absolute power of veto. If he does not want contact between the volunteer and a third person then that is that. If he does then it is still up to the third person to agree or disagree and up to the volunteer to decide whether such contact is appropriate or practicable.

Provided the requirements of confidentiality are met (these will be discussed in chapter 7), it makes no difference which of the parties suggests the contact. The client may wish to involve his wife or co-drinker. The volunteer or agency may be contacted by worried mothers or concerned friends, or the volunteer may herself suggest that expanding her services to other connected people might be beneficial.

How to decide

Assuming that everyone else is in agreement, how then does the volunteer decide what is appropriate and practicable? The answer to this is connected with the initial purpose behind the volunteer-client contact. What did you see yourself as doing in the first place? What was the agreement between you and your client? Is the proposed development in line with that agreement?

It may be that to introduce a third person will increase the likelihood of you and your client achieving your original aims. Or it may be that, in the light of new information or a new state of affairs, you both decide that you need to modify your aims in a significant way. The young man on probation, for example, may decide that although it is important to him to be treated as an equal by you, there are other things which are more important. Perhaps he wants your support while he arrives at a new understanding with his parents about what his relationship is with them. The one may grow out of the other. In such a case a new understanding of what your client needs may lead to a fresh look at whom it is best to involve.

In another situation it may be quite appropriate to

encourage three-, four- or five-way contact if the purpose is to alleviate loneliness. Such contact may also develop new relationship skills between family members. Your client's needs may be better met, ultimately, by forging stronger links with others rather than with yourself. If you are taking a youth fishing you may consider taking his friend, too. That way they may learn to relate to each other as well as to you.

Different considerations would come to bear, though, in cases where your client and his family and friends have similar or parallel needs. It may be better to acknowledge these needs separately. Husband and wife may need to resolve their drink problems separately, receiving support from similarly skilled but different volunteers. Joint victims of the same burglary may both need an understanding ear, but it is hard to listen to two people when one is articulate in his rage and the other paralysed by a sense of almost total helplessness. Even more obviously, the parties to a 'single' matrimonial problem may well need the ear of more than a single volunteer.

Situations such as the above vary, of course, from those situations where the third person's wish to be involved arises from a totally different need or a totally different perception of the situation. In a case such as that proposed earlier, both the delinquent youth and his concerned mother may want three-way contact with the volunteer. But while the boy wants to show off his new 'friend' and ally, the mother wants an ally in her efforts to exercise what she sees as much-needed control over her erring child. Involvement in such a case could clearly lead to conflicts of interest.

The above examples suggest at least some of the considerations to bear in mind when making decisions about the appropriateness of becoming involved with third persons.

Issues to think about

- Who is your client?
- Are his needs better served by involving third persons? Why/why not?
- If so, who, and do they understand and agree with the initial reasons for contact?
- Do the third persons need/want their own volunteers?
- Do you have the time, opportunity and skill to control your involvement in your client's other relationships?

Finally, it is perhaps worth raising two questions you may ask yourself which will help you establish what the purpose of your contact is, how appropriate that purpose is and how well you are achieving what you are trying to do. These questions are:

1 Are you filling a permanent or a temporary gap for your client?
2 Are you displacing someone else in your client's life?

The first part of the chapter looked at how you as a volunteer fit into your client's scheme of things. If you have examined why your client chose you at this point in his life you will know what your job is, how long it is likely to take and how you will know when it is finished. Your contact has some purpose which is likely to make it more manageable and satisfying for you both. The first question above provides another way of helping you focus on what you are doing.

The second part of the chapter looked at how and when you might decide to establish contact with other people who are significant to your client and provides a framework for answering questions about third persons. The second question provides you with a way of checking if your involvement is appropriate. The question is not about *replacing*, but *displacing*. There are times when your job is, appropriately, to fill a gap which has been created by a loss or a change. That is a very different thing from taking over from friends, relatives, acquaintances or professional workers who are already involved.

The point to remember is that so long as your client has *more* opportunities for his needs to be met, given your involvement, you have probably identified your task accurately.

5 Mental and physical health

Mind and body

In your time as a volunteer you will inevitably come across people who are less than healthy. Direct treatment of a health problem is obviously not your responsibility, but our health is an integral part of the way we are and act. Therefore, your client's health will affect the way he will think and feel. Being with a client who is ill, either mentally or physically, involves all the other factors that we have included in this book – emotional ones, practical ones, relationships, and the way you work with professionals.

In this chapter we are going to look at how health problems may influence your client's outlook. It will include how best to help a client come to terms with his own approaching death and how to help family and friends cope with bereavement. We will also consider the support needed by people who care for someone who is ill, disabled or infirm.

Mental health

One of the areas where we are most prone to metaphorically sticking labels on people is in the area of mental health, or rather illness: 'She's got totally neurotic about her work', 'He's gone paranoid about his wife', 'They are really obsessional about keeping the garden tidy'. These are terms that are borrowed from the psychology of Freud, Jung and other psychologists. They are used in an unthinking or short-hand manner to state that the person is behaving in a way that, by our very use of the terms, we deem abnormal. Very few of us could actually say what Freud meant when he used the terms paranoia or neurosis, although we could give our own definition of the terms as we use them. But when you describe someone as neurotic I might say she is worried, or when you say paranoid I might say frightenend.

When we use words that have a slightly mysterious, medical feel to them what we are sometimes doing is saying that this problem is outside our sphere of work. Thus, to describe a man as paranoid about his wife is to imply that there is very little we as laymen can do about it. However, if we throw out the jargon and say the man is frightened that his wife might leave him, a response is called from us. Partially dismissing your client by hanging an ill-defined label on him is to evade at least some of his problem and to create a barrier between you. Perhaps you would not label yourself as paranoid or obsessional. However, there have invariably been times when you have been frightened, insecure or over-concerned about something you have to do. As we have mentioned before, seeing something of yourself in the client is one of the ways of giving the best help you can.

When help is not wanted

A difficult situation you may encounter is where you feel that your client is in need of medical help but there seems to be no way of obtaining it. Either the client does not recognise the need himself or he refuses to seek help, perhaps for fear of what will happen. You need to remember that the client has the right to choose for himself his own course of action. In the event of mental illness, however, he might not have the capacity to judge what is in his own best interests. There is no neat and tidy answer to this problem because there are so many individual factors to take into account:

- Is he a danger to himself?
- Is he a danger to others?
- Can you discern whether his resistance to medical help is because of a fear he has always had or because of a characteristic of his present illness?

You must be clear about what your responsibility is in such a situation:

- Do you have a responsibility?
- Do you have the right to interfere to this extent in your client's life?

- If you do not seek help on his behalf and the situation deteriorates, will you be held responsible by others for what has happened?

Some of these questions you will be able to answer before you get into such a situation because the range of responsibility of your organisation will be clear to you. Others you will need to ask yourself and answer only in the light of a particular set of circumstances. The decision is never easy.

Professional diagnosis

It may be that your client has already had his mental state diagnosed by a doctor. Mental health care and treatment is becoming more community-based. There is an increased likelihood that your agency will come into contact with clients who a few years ago would have been cared for by the state in an institution. This means that you may well have clients coming to you or referred to you who are moderately or severely mentally ill. (There is a long-running debate among the professions as to how one defines mental illness, or if there is such a thing at all. For the purposes of this book we shall use the term to cover that state where the client himself is distressed by what is happening to him. This may be causing a major disturbance to his normal lifestyle.) There are two things that you must be aware of in such a situation – the limits of your own capabilities and the work that is being done by the medical profession for him.

Assessment

When someone is mentally ill it is not always easy to assess what he needs or wants. The process of drawing up a contract with him, telling him what you can and cannot offer, may be difficult if not impossible. It may be that his illness makes him unreliable or inconsistent, his behaviour may be withdrawn or uninhibited. There may be marked mood swings and he may find thinking in a logical and coherent way impossible. There is a sense, then, in which you just have to 'play it by ear.' Take each meeting with your client as it comes and try not to expect more of him than he is capable of managing.

There may be inconsistencies in what he says or does, he may not remember what happened at your last meeting, he may fantasise about past experiences or future expectations. It is not normally your role to point these things out to him.

Contradicting someone who is trying to sort out his own way of interpreting the world or of finding some comfort in it can cause him further distress. But it is possible to give him support and encouragement when he talks of his 'reality' without reinforcing his fantasies.

Your role

It is your role to give the client some of the support that he is probably looking for. This means giving your time to listen to him, when he can talk about whatever he likes without judgement or criticism. And it means giving him support by praising his achievements and sharing his pain. The client may be finding extreme difficulty in expressing what he feels about himself and where he stands in relation to the world around him. It should be your aim to be a part of that world which is warm and caring, accepting of both him and his feelings.

Unfortunately, there is still much social prejudice concerning mental illness. Your client will possibly have been laughed at or made to feel alien – things which can only make his sense of isolation and 'otherness' worse. Your relationship with him can prove to him that although the world can be a cruel and heartless place, there is also warmth and acceptance. The kind of relationship that you will be aiming to provide as a volunteer will be within your capabilities and may be one of the crucial factors in his eventual recovery.

Differences of approach

In chapter 7 we will be looking in some detail at what is involved in working with professionals, but we need to look briefly at this here. It may be that your voluntary work brings you into close contact with professional workers, such as social workers and probation officers, or perhaps you will only meet in very exceptional circumstances, as is the case with the Samaritans. But whatever the degree of contact, the relationship between volunteer and professional should be one that works well for the benefit of the client. You should be aware of differences between your approach and that of the professional.

With regard to clients who are mentally ill, the professionals involved could be psychiatrists, psychologists or community nurses. The mental health care of the client is their responsibility and they have the knowledge and the resources to treat the problem in the most appropriate way. Treatment can be by drugs and/or by setting tasks and goals for the client to achieve. There are two things you should bear in mind:

- You do not have the same knowledge as the professional, either of the treatment in general or the client in particular, neither do you have the same responsibilities
- You should try to become aware of what the goals are that have been set for the client and seek not to undermine them. In other words, you should work with the professionals and not against them, even if you do not understand or agree with them.

Your role is one of befriending the client, which in itself may become an important part of his recovery. The professional's role is to treat the patient, which may or may not include befriending. By working together, even if you have never met, you can help provide the conditions where the client can work through his difficulties and become healthy again.

Issues to think about

- Do you actually know the true meanings of some of the labels you tend metaphorically to stick on people? Write down some of those you most frequently use and try to define them.
- Is it necessary to know theories about mental health in order to help the client? Why or why not?
- What are the most important things you can do for someone who is mentally ill, and how can you tell if you are doing them?

Physical illness

There are two assumptions that most of us make about our futures. Whether it is booking theatre tickets for the weekend or planning next year's holiday, we are assuming both that we will be alive and that we will have the physical capacity to enjoy ourselves. Since you are reading this book it is safe to assume that the first assumption is still holding good, but sometimes the second lets us down. If you catch 'flu or break your ankle tomorrow, you would have to cancel the theatre. That is annoying and slightly frustrating, but you know it is not the end of the world and you can probably manage to keep it in perspective. Next week or next month you expect to be fully fit again and that, after all, is the main thing. But some of your clients will be coming to you because the assumptions they have made about themselves have been contradicted by the facts. They know that they will not be well again for some time, if ever again. And for them that, after all, is the main thing.

Expectations

Being physically ill affects not only what a person can do but also what he feels. He expected that his life would continue as most lives do, that he would support his family, enjoy his spare time, eventually retire and take the grandchildren fishing. Now his life has deviated from that expectation and he must come to terms with two major emotional changes:

- First he has to cope with the way the illness is making him feel now – the pain, fear, loss of confidence, uncertainty and insecurity.
- Then he has to work out a strategy for coping with the illness so that he can still get as much as possible out of life. He will either want to return to some of his original expectations of himself or, where that is not possible, he has to work out new goals and satisfactions.

The client may also have practical difficulties to sort out. Giving up playing football can be as devastating to one person as giving up his job to another. But often it is the small things that hurt the most, like not being able to pick up the children or walk round the supermarket. And then there are the worries of where the money is going to come from while he is ill, how is he going to pay the mortgage, what will happen if . . . In addition to this the illness itself may be causing immense practical problems, such as how to deal with a colostomy or a wheelchair, how to communicate in a new way, how to know when he is pushing himself too hard.

Reducing the isolation

Being ill is losing control, over your life, your body, your hopes. It is something like having your house burgled or being sent to prison, but it comes from within and can be more difficult to cope with because of that. The memory of having your house burgled usually loses its emotional potency after a period of time; in prison there are hundreds of other people in exactly the same situation. Being ill is often being isolated, from your expectations of your future, from other people, from a part of yourself.

Only the person suffering knows what it feels like, both physically and emotionally, what battles he has already fought and what there are in the future. He may doubt his capabilities to cope with the future. Saying 'I know how you feel' is often not true – you do not know how someone else really feels, and the assumption that you do can be offensive to the client. Saying 'I am sorry this is happening to you' is nearer the truth and encourages him to tell you more about how he is feeling.

Accepting decisions

When we are ill we tend to think that no one else has suffered in quite the way that we have, but when other people are ill we think we know just what they are going through. That is, the way we cope with illness is the way we feel other people should cope with it as well. Some people just want to be left on their own, others want to have people around them. There is the choice between taking all the medicine possible in order to keep the symptoms at bay, or taking the minimum possible in order to keep your body free from drugs. Some people will accept whatever their doctor tells them, while others will seek differing opinions and other methods of treatment. Whatever options we choose for ourselves tend to be the ones we expect or encourage other people to opt for. Accepting that your client may make decisions about the management of his illness or the future course of his life that you would not have made for him may be difficult.

If your client has had a time in hospital, he will have been told what to do and when to do it, in the nicest way possible, of course. But there are very few decisions that a hospital patient can make for himself. When he goes home, or if he has always been at home, he will have instructions to follow, things he must and must not do. The professionals' contact with the client is very different from yours because you have very different responsibilities. Doctors, of necessity, treat their patients as 'cases', to be cured because the pressure of both time and resources precludes anything else. A good bedside manner is an efficient way of covering this underlying truth. The support and befriending of the whole person, but not the treatment of the illness, is your responsibility.

Your role

The client will have talked to the doctor about his medical

condition, to the nurse about the management of his illness
and perhaps to the social worker about practical and financial
changes to be made. So why you? Possibly you are the only
person to whom he can talk about himself. The only person,
that is, who sees him as a whole person and not as a set of
problems to find answers for. By allowing him to talk about his
fears, pain and sense of helplessness, you are helping him to
feel less isolated and more in control. Illness, almost by
definition, tends to be a self-absorbing thing. The client may
need to try out ideas and theories on you to find out what he
really feels and thinks, or he may need you just to be there to
hold his hand while he copes with the pain.

Pain, disability and the unpredictability of some illnesses can
be very frightening, not only for the sufferer but for the
people who are with him. You may find yourself visiting the
client for an hour and spending another hour standing by the
front door while his wife or children tell you what his illness is
doing to them. Their expectations also have to change and
strains can be put on relationships that need to be
acknowledged and dealt with. Allowances have to be made for
the person who is ill and extra attention given to him. This can
make other members of the household feel neglected,
burdened and perhaps resentful.

As has been stressed throughout this book, yours is not to
do but to listen. It is very tempting to whip out your
metaphorical spanner and try to mend relationships that are
strained and cracking. The solution may be very easy for you
to see but you have to let people make their own decisions and
reach their own conclusions, otherwise you are just another
person who is coming along and taking control away from them.
The result is that people can feel more isolated if the supposed
solution does not work; they could lose their trust in you and
feel that they are back with no one who really understands.

By allowing all the people involved to talk to you, should
they want to, you are enabling them to work out their feelings
and to reach their own conclusions. The fact that they are
husband and wife does not make confidentiality less important.
If one is telling you something that you feel the other should
know, do not take it upon yourself to be the informer. You
should be encouraging all the family to talk to each other, not
to talk through you.

Effects on you

Another aspect to be considered is that being with someone

who is in great physical pain may also have its effect upon you. Pain is a frightening thing, so it is reasonable to be frightened by it, regardless of whether it is your own pain or that of someone else. However, you are not going to help your client if every time he groans a look of horror comes on your face. If you are fairly sure you will not be able to cope with your client's pain, admit it. It really is not something to be ashamed of. Your agency should be sensitive and caring enough of both you and the client to arrange for someone else to be with the client.

If you can manage to stick it out and share the pain with your client, do not dismiss its effects on you with 'Well, it wasn't me who was actually feeling it.' Of course it is going to affect you and you need to look after yourself. Just because the client cannot get away from his pain does not mean that you cannot seek relief for yourself when you need to. It is not a form of betrayal or weakness, it is a means of ensuring that the next time you are with him, and the next after that, you will be able to cope in the same way and give him what he needs while you are there.

Issues to think about

- How do you deal with your feelings of helplessness when you are with someone who is in great pain?
- How does it affect the support you give a client if he makes a decision about his future which you think is wrong?
- Does another person's pain make you angry? If so, how do you deal with that constructively?
- What are the positive things that can come out of a long period of illness for a) the client and b) you?

Death

Life has a habit of rising up and striking us with the knowledge of our own mortality. We have a near miss while driving the car, a sudden pain in the chest, we read of the death of someone our own age or younger. But those things soon pass and we get on with the far more pleasurable business of living our lives. For some of us, ceasing to be in this world is unimaginable and frightening, while for others the thought of death is acceptable but the process of dying is the thing to be feared. Yet because we all have to die, because we really have no choice in the matter anyway, we tend not to talk about our fears. One of the things you are going to have to ask yourself as a volunteer is whether or not you can bear to listen to a client talking about death. As with any other situation when you are with a client, it is not your feelings that are important, at least for the time that you are with him. If you are not able to control your fears about death and dying when with the client you run the danger of doing him harm.

Emotional reactions

If your client has been told that his illness is terminal he will be feeling a whole range of emotions, either simultaneously or consecutively. Some of these can be fear, anger, disbelief, anxiety about the people close to him, depression and grief. He may show a determination to fight against all the odds or he may be accepting and passive. He might show large mood swings between wanting to get the best out of the life remaining to him and staring into space just waiting for death to come. Some people feel a sense of relief when they know their death is not far away and this can make them feel guilty. There will be nothing you can do to prevent your client from dying (unless he is considering suicide), but you can do a tremendous amount to make his death easier.

People sometimes have a tendency to behave like an electricity fuse-box – when there is an overload the mind and/or emotions switch off for a while. This can happen when someone is told he is going to die in that there may be a period of denial. The client might be able to tell you quite dispassionately what he has been told, or he might have totally blanked it out of his mind and talk about his still unaltered plans for the future. You will not help him by pointing the above process out to him – what he is doing is giving himself time. Once he has acknowledged what is happening to him, time is the thing he will not have. This can be a very difficult period for the people who love him and who know what is happening. They are starting to grieve but are having their grief contradicted by his behaviour. This is the time of false hopes and not knowing what to believe. Your involvement should be neutral, not building up and reinforcing hopes and dreams, but not smashing them either.

Coping with grief

If someone whom we love is going away, whether for two weeks or two years, we sometimes have a sense of anticipatory loss. We try to remember every word they say and how they say it, every expression on their faces, how they walk and laugh. The same is true for someone who is dying; he will anticipate the parting from the people around him and experience grief because they will soon be lost to him. But this process may also be taking place in the people who are closest to him. This can mean that their times together are both highly charged emotionally and very intense, with the result that they can also be a great strain. For the person dying it can be an enormous relief to have someone to whom he can talk who cares enough to be there but does not have the same intensity of feeling. If this is so, it gives him a great freedom to express what he really feels instead of having to hide his fear or anxiety for the sake of his family or friends. You can act as a safety valve for your client, giving him both the strength to face what is happening to him and the courage to face the changing relationships between him and his family.

Even though you will probably not have the same emotional attachment to your client, this does mean that it may only be to you that he expresses his deepest feelings. That is very hard on you, especially when the most probable end to it will be with the client's death. This is one of those situations when you will call on all your expertise as a counsellor and yet it will still be difficult. You will have to:

- be open to the client and encourage him to express his feelings
- cope with the feelings raised in you on a personal level
- guard against protecting yourself by becoming defensive with the client because of his pain and coming death
- come into contact with his family and close friends when they also need someone to talk to and with whom they can share their true feelings

This is not going to be easy for you but, apart from seeking adequate support for yourself, you should also keep in mind that by your presence you are making a difficult period in your client's life easier. You cannot make the problem go away and you cannot ease the physical symptoms, but you do have the opportunity to do the most important thing for your client, and that is to make his dying easier.

The importance of time

It is likely that you will have experienced grief yourself at some time. There is an enormous sense of loss, not only for the person who has died but also in your own life – there is now a hole in it that you feel will never be filled. The future looks cold and bleak, perhaps the source of some of your strength in facing life has gone and you do not know how you are going to find that strength on your own. Initially there can be a sense of shock and numbness, even if the death has been expected. There are the immediate practical problems surrounding the funeral and perhaps long-term ones of changed income, the necessity to move house and what furniture and personal possessions to dispose of.

What the grieving person needs in the midst of all this is the opportunity to do just that – grieve. All too often this opportunity is taken away too soon. For example, the man who has lost his wife has perhaps lost the most important part of his life, the person around whom his life revolved and the person who gave his life meaning. For his friends and neighbours the death is something to grieve about initially, but then other aspects of their own lives regain their previous importance. The husband, who had people around him who were also grieving at the time of the death, now has no one with whom to share his feelings. He can see that their lives have returned to normal while his has not, so he hides his feelings and pretends he is recovering faster than he is. What he needs is someone to give him the time to talk, to cry and to rage, if that is what he needs. He also needs the freedom to decide for himself when the grieving is over, as far as it will ever be, not have it imposed upon him by someone limiting the time for him, whether consciously or not.

It should therefore be clear what your role is. Grief takes time to heal and that time is different for everyone. The most important things that you can give your client are time, patience, understanding and acceptance of what he is feeling. He needs to feel unhurried and to feel that he can trust you not to be bored as he talks again and again of what the person who has died meant to him. It could be of profound importance to him to know that, perhaps a year or two after the event, there is at least one person who knows what he is still feeling and understands why.

Issues to think about

- If you have had periods of grief in your own life, what were the things you most needed from other people?
- How can you best help a client to come to terms with his grief?

- What would you find the most difficult aspects of being with a client who is dying?

Caring for the carers

(Although the comments below are centred around caring for someone who is physcially ill, in general they apply to all those who care for someone or something else such as parents for their children, the person committed to his work, the pet owner.)

At some point in our adult lives all of us need someone to look after us, even if we do submit to it with bad grace and resent the circumstances. For most of us the illness passes and we take over the responsibility for looking after ourselves again. On the other hand we may become the carers – if your partner has a bad dose of 'flu you look after him with the knowledge that you will not be running up and down the stairs with trays for very long. Whether being cared for or caring, the length of time is an important factor in our acceptance and ability to withstand the strain.

In contrast to this, an increasing number of people either choose or are thrust into the role of long-term carers. A few decades ago it was fairly standard practice to send a handicapped, chronically ill or confused relative off to an institution to be looked after by someone else. Nowadays there is pressure for the reverse to happen – for people to be sent from hostels, homes and hospitals back to their families. In these circumstances their relatives may take on the role of 24-hour nurse, pharmacist, psychiatrist, cleaner, launderer and caterer, because 'There is nowhere else for him to go', or 'We couldn't bear the thought of him in a home', or 'He gave me 20 years of his life so I owe him something.'

The desire to look after a relative, whether a handicapped child or a confused mother-in-law, generated from love, loyalty and/or duty can be severely threatened by the realities of what that caring entails and its consequences for the carer's life. The threat is much greater if the carer is entering into the role with reluctance, perhaps because she feels she has no other choice.

Consequences of commitment

A large number of carers find looking after a relative a rewarding, life-enhancing experience which gives them satisfaction, purpose and a sense of fulfilment. These people

are unlikely to become your clients unless they are going
through a temporary period of added strain for some reason.
But some people find that by devoting a large part of their
lives to someone else their own lives are affected in a negative
way. Examples of these are:

- feelings of mental and physical tiredness from which there
  is no respite
- loneliness because there is no escape from the house for
  long enough to make a life of their own
- love for the relative being overtaken by feelings of
  resentment and anger
- inability to respond to demands being made by other
  members of the family
- the knowledge that a number of opportunities, either large
  or small, in the carer's life, have had to be passed by because
  of this all-consuming commitment

Those feelings are very difficult to admit to oneself, let alone
talk about. In the supermarket or at the doctor's, the carer will
be asked by acquaintances how her mother/son/husband is,
and she will give the polite answer. It would be impossible to
stand by the check-out or within the hearing of the doctor's
receptionist and say how she was up all night, had been so
tired and angry that she had hit her mother this morning, and
how she is feeling intense guilt and shame – as well as
tiredness, resentment and depression.

Sharing the consequences

We all have feelings and reactions that we are ashamed of and
think that nobody else has. Only in talking about them and
sharing them with others can we see that they are a normal
reaction to a sometimes intolerable situation. Hitting one's
mother can rarely be the right thing to do but the strains,
tensions and feelings which led up to that action are usually
entirely understandable. However, the feelings of guilt about
the physical action may be generalised into feeling guilty
because of 'not coping' very well with the whole situation.
Your role will be to supply the care and support for the carer,
in a non-judgemental, un-shockable, empathising way, which
she needs in order to sort out her feelings.
  Carers often appear to be energetic, efficient people who
pack more into one day than the rest of us do into five. But
you need to be able to recognise the signs of someone who is

not waving but drowning. They are not easy to generalise or define, and often it is 'gut-feeling' that you have to go on. In chapter 8 we will be looking at how you must look after yourself. You could take the things mentioned there and apply them to the carer:

- Is she enjoying herself?
- Is she obviously so tired that she is frightened to stop in case she cannot get started again?
- Has she become overly single minded about the tasks she has set herself to do?
- Has the scope and range of her life narrowed down to just the person she is caring for?
- Does she answer all questions about herself by telling you how her mother is feeling?

You will have to give the carer a lot of time. She is unlikely to tell you of the resentment and anger at your first meeting. She needs to be able to feel that she can trust you and may test you out on other less important matters first. Once she has started to let go, perhaps for the first time in years, she is going to need a large amount of support from you. Her situation is not one that she can walk away from, so she has to go on dealing with it while at the same time working out what her emotions are and perhaps modifying them.

What she does not need is judgement, criticism, or someone to point out her errors and failures. She will be only too aware of those herself. There are rarely immediate, easy solutions, so the support you give may go on for some time and will probably be making considerable demands on you. If you are the only person the carer is confiding in you need to be aware of the danger of her becoming dependent on you and the consequences of that if it happens. Both you and the carer must come to some agreement about how your relationship is going to develop and eventually come to an end. Pages 36–7 will help you in thinking about this.

When things change

It may be that the person being cared for dies. This may leave a devastating hole in the carer's life. For years she has ordered her life around routines, demands and needs other than her own. Suddenly they are not there any more. It can be disorientating and frightening, and the carer will need help both to grieve and to recognise her life – two major tasks to be gone through at the same time. Again there may be guilt, this time at the feelings of relief and release at the other person's death.

You need to be clear about your role in such a situation. You cannot fill the hole in the carer's life and should not try. What you can do is help her to build a life of her own by encouraging her to put into practice the things that she would like for herself. She may decide to start going to church again or take up ballroom dancing. By all means support her in what she decides, and perhaps accompany her on her first steps out into the world, but be aware of the danger of becoming a buffer instead of a bridge between her and the world.

As with all the situations mentioned in this book, caring for carers is about listening, empathising, being non-judgemental and supportive. The difference is that where you can see that there will be an end to some situations, i.e. a probation order or a marriage breakdown, caring for someone can go on for years and decades. Dealing with the situation is not your responsibility, but dealing with the emotions raised by that situation might be. It is an important distinction to make for it gives a possible end to the contract you make with your client, whether overt or not. The emotional issues may be resolved even though the situation will carry on.

Issues to think about

- How would you/do you feel about looking after a member of your family whom you do not get on with?
- Is it possible to deal with only the emotional side of the carer's life? Give reasons why/why not.
- Could there ever be a time when the carer's feeling must come first, regardless of the consequences for the person being cared for? Give examples.

6 Establishing the right relationship with your client

In any relationship between two people there are dimensions to that relationship other than those which people are aware of on an immediate, conscious level. Some of these are present right from the beginning of the relationship, some develop as the relationship itself develops. An obvious example is body language, parts of which we are aware of but a lot of which registers in an unconscious way. As the relationship develops we can quickly define the body language of the other person and see in it nuances and facets that we were blind to at first. Like any other language, we have to learn it.

This chapter is going to consider some of the things that happen in a relationship, either explicitly or implicitly, other than the 'surface' activities of listening and talking, giving support and comfort. Most of what we shall discuss concerns the things that may go wrong in the relationship. When things are going well there is not the same need to analyse the factors involved to see how they can be changed. The knowledge that things are going well and that the client is gaining a great deal from the time with you is a wonderful thing to have. By considering what happens when things go wrong you can seek to avoid such circumstances and gain that knowledge more easily.

Where and when

It is easier to talk with someone in a comfortable, quiet room than it is on the platform of Victoria railway station. What is not so obvious is the dynamics of 'your place or mine'. If the client comes to the place where you normally work as a volunteer, that in itself gives you a large amount of control. For you the room will be familiar, as are the noises coming from the rest of the building or outside. For the client it is strange and needs some getting used to. You are on familiar territory, for him it is unfamiliar, which immediately puts him at a disadvantage. It is also possible that there is a telephone nearby, which it may be your responsiblity to answer. If this is so, you need to make it clear to the client that you will have to leave him if the telephone rings and it is as disturbing for you as it is for him.

You also control the social niceties: when to offer coffee, which chair to direct him to sit in, how warm to have the room. A proportion of all polite behaviour is actually a socially acceptable technique for putting the other person at a disadvantage. You need to be aware of these things and work out how you can present not only yourself, but also your surroundings in as unthreatening way as possible.

The reverse is true if you visit the client in his home. You need to remind yourself that although it may be important for your client to feel he is in control, for you that is not so important. Your chief consideration is how the client is feeling. Where you set about finding that out is not vital for you.

Type of referral

The client may initiate the contact with you, by telephoning the Samaritans or walking into the citizens advice bureau office, or he may be referred to you by someone else. This second situation occurs when someone is referred to Victim Support or sent to the Probation Service by the courts. The first type can be called self-referral, the second automatic referral. Some organisations are a mixture of these, for example a cancer support group where some people will come of their own accord and some be referred by their doctor. The crucial difference between the two is that in self-referral the client has come to you because he wants help, whereas in automatic referral you go to the client when he may not want and may even reject your help. Except in the Probation Service, there is not a great deal you can do about this, other than let the person know he can contact you should he change his mind. This sort of thing is obviously discouraging if it happens too often, as far as your work as a volunteer is concerned, but there are two positive aspects to it as far as the client is concerned:

- He now knows of your existence and what you can offer so he can always come back to you at a later date.
- It is only by pursuing a policy of automatic referral that the agency can also pick up the cases where their help is needed and is of great benefit to the client.

Issues to think about

- How does the way the client is referred to you make a difference to your relationship?
- Does it make any difference to you whether you see the client in his home or your office? If so, what?

Frame of mind

As you become more familiar with the work you do and the demands it makes on you, an easy trap to fall into is thinking you can do it standing on your head. The truth is that if you do fall into such a mood of complacency you will not be the best volunteer you could be. While you are with the client he needs, and perhaps has a right to expect, your full attention. If you allow things to distract you while you are with him you will not be giving him your full attention and it may be he will notice.

The art of 'being with' someone is difficult to cultivate. If he needs to sit in silence for some time, it is very easy for your mind to wander to composing the shopping list or wondering what to make for tea. His need, however, is to feel that you are with him, even in the silence, sharing his pain, frustration or whatever. This will take an enormous amount of concentration from you and as a result is demanding and draining. When he is talking you need to concentrate on all that he says in order to pick up the significance of what he is saying, sometimes in the insignificant, 'throw away' comment.

You will not be able to do this unless you have put yourself in the right frame of mind. There is both a practical and an emotional side to this.

First, if you have left the car on a one-hour parking space and you find that your time with the client is going to be longer than this, you will be distracted by thoughts of traffic wardens. Practical details like this are easily remedied, although there are others where all you can do is give yourself the time to leave them alone for a while. If you have to make an appointment, if you must collect a coat from the dry cleaners, give yourself far more leeway between what you estimate will be the end of your time with the client, or the beginning, and the time you have set for these other things.

·Second, very few of us have completely even emotional lives. There are days when we have an argument, are made very angry, or are elated at a piece of good news. Fate usually decrees that these will be the days when you have to see a client. Sometimes it is impossible to switch off the emotions, so then it may be appropriate to consider whether you will be doing your client much good, or even positive harm, by seeing him. If that is the case, cancelling the appointment or asking someone else to take over from you is the best thing to do for both your client and yourself.

Setting your feelings aside

Most of the time we are able to set our feelings aside for a short while, but when seeing a client this needs to be done by a definite decision rather than speculative optimism. You need to say to yourself, 'The client is here, I will forget about my anger/frustration/new grandchild for a while and concentrate upon him.' What you should not say is, 'I hope the client distracts me enough to keep my mind off other things.' That would be a misuse of both the client and the time you have together.

Whether your distractions are of an emotional or practical nature, what we are really saying is that you must reduce your own level of anxiety to a minimum. Learning how to cope with traffic wardens or talking to someone else about your own feelings before you see the client is one way of doing this. The other is to discipline your mind to control your feelings for the duration of the time you are with the client. If you can do neither of these things, you must consider alternatives to seeing your client at that particular time.

Red-flag listening

We all have areas of 'red-flag' listening, where hearing someone else talk about a particular subject sets off a response in us which is either disproportionate or inappropriate. For example, if a member of your family has been murdered, listening to a murderer talking about his view of things might be extremely difficult for you. You should recognise which are your particular subjects and either avoid them as far as you can or learn to modify your reactions. We are not saying that you should not involve yourself in areas where you have personal experience or strong feelings, but that you should recognise the circumstances where these expectations and feelings prejudice your outlook.

Issues to think about

- How does the frame of mind that you are in affect what help you can give the client? What can you do about it?
- What are your areas of red-flag listening? How can you modify them?

Transference and projection

These two things are most likely to happen when your relationship with the client has become fairly well established and he has come to know and trust you quite well. Indeed, it is probably because he has come to trust you, in the sense that he can safely show his anger, fear or hurt, that he can allow himself to experiment with these two processes. The two terms are best defined by giving examples.

Transference

Suppose a client has come to you because he has just been through a particularly difficult divorce. And suppose that one of the things he could not do at the time of the divorce was express how angry he was with his wife. Perhaps his own feelings of guilt prevented it, or he was frightened of losing control, or he was hanging on in the hope that they could patch things up. As your relationship with him develops, so will his trust in you and his sense of being accepted by you. In other words, you create a safe area where he can be himself. As you both explore his feelings in more depth, he will begin to rediscover his anger. As we explained earlier, emotions need an object. If your client has never expressed his anger to his wife because he has never felt safe enough to do so, he may express his anger to you, using you as the object, because with you he feels safe.

Your client may, therefore, become suddenly and seemingly unreasonably angry with you, either for no apparent reason or by exaggerating some small fault on your part out of all proportion. Although it may be hard for you to take and absorb, you should not react to his anger by becoming angry yourself. He is, in fact, giving you his anger to absorb and take away. If you refuse it by becoming angry with him, or by rejecting him in some way, you are denying him what he needs. In some part, you are breaking the trust which you have both worked at developing.

It sometimes happens that once the client has gone through this process of transference he can look back and see for himself what he has done. In calmness he realises that his anger was misdirected and he will know why he has done it. He will also need to know that you understand what has been going on. Or it may be that he will want to leave his anger with you and walk away from it. If you are someone he knows he will not see again, it is quite safe for him to let his feelings emerge, knowing that there will be no repercussions. Your problem will be that you have absorbed whatever he is feeling without knowing how it has helped him afterwards. Again, you should make sure there is someone with whom you can talk it over in order that his feelings do not stay with you.

Anger is not the only emotion which can be transferred, although it is possibly the most common. One of the most difficult to deal with is love, where the client has loved someone in the past and then transfers that loving to you. Great awareness is needed on your part to treat the client sensitively and sympathetically while minimising the sense of rejection at his love being refused. It is almost impossible to get this sort of situation right. You have to encourage the relationship to develop in terms of making the counselling process more effective, but discourage the client from transferring his feelings to you. You will have to think very hard about whether you are the right person to carry on the counselling relationship with him.

When deep emotions have been bottled up for a long time, transference can be a very effective means of release. It requires wisdom and experience on your part to recognise when this is happening. Your role is one of enormous help and benefit to the client. You should not feel personally threatened by what is happening nor let if affect your relationship with the client. You must also ensure that you have adequate support from your colleagues.

Projection

If we have performed a task which is open to inspection by other people we expect praise if we have done it well, censure if we have done it badly. It is quite likely that among your clients there will be some who feel that no matter what they do, or however hard they try, they will never get things right. They will therefore expect other people to censure them.

Suppose you have a client who can see very little good in himself. His self-confidence and self-esteem will be very low, he will dislike himself and he will feel that he is a failure in a number of ways. He will expect that other people will hold this opinion of him, and this will include you. Therefore he will assume you also find him unloveable, a failure and not worth spending much time on. The client has projected his own feelings about himself on to you and will be expecting to see them reflected back. These feelings may have been with the client for many years and be an integral part of the structure he uses to make sense of the world. If he is a failure no one will be expecting him to have a high-flying job. He does not expect it either, therefore there is little point in having ambitions or high hopes.

People who have been through some traumatic experience can lose their sense of self-confidence and self-esteem for a while. They look back on their past achievements and feel they will never be able to do anything like it again. They may be having trouble coping with their on-going commitments, and again will be expecting that the whole world can see their failure to come to terms with their lives and be holding them up to ridicule.

Whereas with transference you accept whatever the client tells you, with projection there is a sense in which you have to fight him. In some way or other, and probably not as directly as this, he will say to you, 'I know you think I am a failure, unloveable and not worth your time.' Your task is to show him, by your words and actions, that you disagree with his evaluation of himself. One way is simply by being there and giving him your time, gentle and repeated contradiction is another. Pointing out to him, in terms which he can understand, that what he is doing is projection can be of great benefit. This is done by taking his statements or assumptions about what he thinks you are thinking, and asking him to give his reasons for what he is saying. You can then carefully explain that what he is saying is wrong and your impression of him is far more positive than is his own.

If your client has been feeling like this for a long time, the process of letting go of one self-image and forming another is long, slow and painful. You will find that you have to say the same positive things about him over and over again until he can reach the stage where he actually believes them for himself.

It follows, then, that for you the process is also long and difficult. You need to be sensitive, gentle and persistent and not lose hope when all you are saying seems to make little difference. There may be times when you get exasperated with him because the positive things you are saying seem perfectly obvious to you but incomprehensible to him. One of the most rewarding things in counselling is to see a client change from believing himself to be bad or worthless to seeing himself as good and of value. Your persistence will be well rewarded.

Issues to think about

- When you have transferred your feelings about one situation on to another? How did this make you feel?
- What are the most effective ways of dealing with projection?

Manipulation

One of the reasons for establishing a contract with your client is so that he knows what he can expect. You may at some time, however, come across a client who tries to push you into giving something other than what is on offer. This can take the overt form of 'I want you to . . .' or can be covert, as in 'If you did this I would feel so much better, and that is what you want, isn't it?'

We tend to think of manipulation as something that is not 'quite right', that is, a means of getting our own way which is slightly underhand. But it can be used in a positive way, where it is an effective means of expression and is used as a tool to bring about some positive gain.

Fantasy

One way of doing this is by the use of fantasy. Some fantasies are obviously unhealthy and in the long-term destructive, but others can have a useful purpose. If a client is feeling an acute sense of grief because he has suddenly realised how much of his life has passed without him having achieved much, he may have difficulty in finding ways of expressing this. Indeed, he may be overwhelmed by grief without knowing why. He may then construct a fantasy/fiction in which, say, his son has died in a car accident. This then gives an object to his grief. Since the sudden death of a close relative is accepted as being an occasion when help and support are given, it is a means of getting the attention he needs for himself. You are then being manipulated by the client into giving support when the factual events are not real. But the sense of grief is real and is the most important thing to the client.

If someone tells us something that is not true, we generally feel a sense of offence, if not outrage. But occasionally it can be the only way in which the client can express his true feelings. Sometimes you have to allow yourself to be manipulated. If you do discover that your client has fantasised much of what he has told you, you must be very careful in your reaction. For him it may have been the means by which he could express himself, and you should probably take it on that level, too – that is, it is probably not the time for moral rectitude. You should stress the positive side of what he has achieved, which is that he has managed to share his feelings with someone. Now he has done this once, perhaps he can do it another time without the need to fantasise.

The negative side

On the other hand, manipulation – where the client is trying to use you, in the pejorative sense – is generally to be resisted, albeit gently. It is a fine line between doing something for the client because you can see that it needs to be done and the client cannot do it for himself, and doing something because the client claims he cannot do it for himself. Sometimes you can sense the difference, sometimes you walk right into the trap. In either case, both you and the client need to refer back to the aims of your organisation and the terms of your contract in order to define what the limits of your involvement are. If the client is set on manipulating you he will not take too kindly to this, but in the long term you can only do the job that you set out to do and if this is not enough for him, he must look elsewhere for what he wants.

Violence

There is one form of manipulation that can be particularly difficult to deal with, and that is one of verbal or physical violence. If the client has tried to manipulate you into doing something, and you have refused, he may resort to threats of one kind or another. Whether he is trying to abuse you verbally or physically, your reaction should be either to get yourself out of the situation as quickly as possible or, if that is not possible, to stand your ground in an unthreatening way.

If you suspect that the situation may get a little heated

before you enter it, provide yourself with back-up. If you are seeing the client in the place where you work from, this could be in the form of having someone nearby who is alert to what might happen and will come to your assistance quickly. If you are visiting the client in his home, take someone else with you or, if that is not possible, make sure that you can get out of the house quickly, that is, stand by the door. And if the situation is really worrying you, do not go. Because you are a volunteer, it does not follow that you have to put up with treatment you do not want to put up with or which places you in danger.

If a situation becomes violent without warning, there are things which you can do to try to ease the tension. Do not react to the client's anger or frustration with anger yourself – it is just like pouring petrol on a bonfire. Ask him why he is angry, what he hopes to achieve by it, whether he would like a cup of tea, anything to get him talking on a calm and reasonable level. It is likely that he will come out with some choice expressions and opinions on your own character or appearance. If you react to these, hurtful though they may be, he will feel he is winning and carry on. If you can absorb the anger and show him that you are accepting his behaviour without being intimidated by it, he will eventually give up trying to manipulate you by it. You should try to stay physically relaxed and if he gets up and walks around the room, stay seated – he is less likely to hit someone who is sitting at a lower level than he is.

Unfortunately, if you take up voluntary counselling work you must accept that there is a fair chance that at some time you will be involved in threatening or violent situations. Acceptance of this will make it less surprising when it does happen and therefore leaves you more equipped to deal with the situation.

Your manipulation

The other side of your relationship is that there is a sense in which you manipulate the client, whether in the form of bringing the interview to a close because it suits you, or in more subtle ways than that. For example, we have talked about how the process of transference works and how the client might do it without realising what he is doing. You, however, do know what is happening and this gives you an advantage over the client. You have much more of an ability to stand outside the situation and view what is going on in an objective, detached manner. This means that, just as the client can try to manipulate you to get what he wants, so you can manipulate the client. Since you are there because you want to be there, it is to be assumed that you would use this to the benefit of your client rather than the benefit of yourself. However, from time to time perhaps you will need to use the chance to detach yourself from the situation in order to review what it is that you are doing to the client as well as what he is doing to himself and to you.

Issues to think about

• Why might someone tell you something that is not true?
• How do you react when you are physically threatened? Does this behaviour need to be modified when you are with a potentially violent client? If so, what kinds of modifications are needed?

Physical contact

So far we have talked about how clients use words and silence to express how they are feeling, and about how you use words and silence to encourage and support them. There can be times, however, when the most effective thing you can do is to hold his hand or put your arms around him.

In some countries and for some people, physical contact between adults is an everyday occurrence that is not considered an intrusion or a presumption. For others it is something that rarely happens but can be sorely missed, especially if they are feeling hurt and lonely. Our twentieth century lifestyle has something to do with this, in that we live in less close proximity to other people and social contacts tend to have a formal element in them. Thus we live in physical isolation where, if we do not have a sexual relationship, physical contact is uncommon, at least on an informal basis. Thus it becomes more difficult both to offer and receive a hand to hold or the famous shoulder to cry on. So much is written and spoken about sexual contact that there is a fear that any physical approach will be misinterpreted as a sexual advance, which also proves to be a great inhibiting factor.

If your client is expressing deeply-felt emotions, perhaps for the first time, he may be feeling vulnerable, lost and a little frightened. He may also only be able to express how he feels by tears. At such a time the most effective thing you can do, and the most effective way you have of letting the client know that you are trying to share some of what he feels, is to hold his hand or put your arms around him. Not only is this a very physical action, it is also symbolic – you will be making him feel safe for a little while and be making him feel secure and less vulnerable simply because you are close and protective.

Physical contact requires sensitivity and courage on your part. You should be able to sense when the right moment is to offer it and be able to do it in an unthreatening way. You are probably going to get it wrong at times because different clients will have different levels of acceptance of your physical nearness. There will be some clients who will not want you physically close to them at all, no matter what the degree of their distress. You need courage to overcome your own inhibitions, to risk being misinterpreted and to risk being rejected.

Even if the need is there, you will not be able to offer all your clients physical contact. If you are a 30-year-old female volunteer with a 30-year-old male client, even if both of you are aware that the contact is for comfort and support only, and even if your actions are not misinterpreted at the time, they are open to misinterpretation later as both you and the client remember what has happened. You may be able to accept it as a normal part of your role as a counsellor, but for the client it may be the first time a woman has held him for a long time. At the time he may be able to accept it as just that, but later he may speculate on what might have happened or what might have been your motives, however erroneously. That is a situation, whether real or potential, which you should avoid.

Issues to think about

- What are your inhibitions about physical contact?
- What are the situations where you would not offer physical contact?

Breakdowns

All of us like some people more than others, and often this is simply because of the way they appear, not because of anything they have said or done. Sometimes we take an unreasonable dislike to someone which we cannot base on anything factual. It is just a feeling. As a volunteer it is probable that you will not be able to choose your clients; you accept them as they walk through the door or you are given a name and address to visit. So it may happen at some point that you meet a client with whom you are supposed to form a caring and supportive relationship and you just do not like him.

There are two alternatives: either you persevere in the hope that you can overcome your initial reaction, or you give up and pass the case to someone else. If you decide to persevere, you must be sure that your feelings are not going to get in the way of what you can offer to the client. If your role is largely one of passive listening, this may not be too difficult. However, when it seems that the befriending may last a fairly long time and therefore make more demands on you, you must be sure at the outset that you can stay the course. If you decide that there is a chance your reaction to the client will affect what he can get out of the relationship, you should be able to hand him over to someone else without him realising what is the reason for the change. There should be no reason for you to tell him that you do not like him – it would serve no purpose at all.

It is just as possible that the reverse will happen and the client will not like you, only he might not be so hesitant to say so. You need to decide whether it really is you he does not like or if it is what you are saying to him or making him think about. If the latter is the case little will be achieved by handing him over to someone else because the problem is with him, not you. It will take skilful handling on your part to bring the client to the point where he can see this, and in doing so you run the risk of the relationship breaking down completely. If it is, however, that you are not the right person for the client there is no shame in admitting this. The client has come to your agency, or been referred to it, because of what the agency has to offer. If the client cannot accept it from you personally he might be able to accept it from someone else. It can be a difficult thing to accept that the agency can sometimes run better if you remove yourself from the scene temporarily.

When the client goes

Sometimes a relationship can break down part way through a befriending. In this case it is unlikely to be your personality that is at fault, but rather that the client has reached a stage where he has to confront something difficult or painful. Rather than face that he may decide to vote with his feet and end the relationship. Although you may feel that you were just beginning to get somewhere, in most circumstances it is up to the client to end the befriending if he wants to. Or it may be that the breakdown comes from your side in that something else is happening in your life that makes it impossible for you to continue to see the client. In this case you will have the difficult task of extricating yourself without letting the client feel you are rejecting him. Explaining as fully as you can what is going on will help, as will you introducing him to the person who is going to take over from you.

Relationships break down for a variety of reasons, but if you are doing everything you can there is no reason for you to feel you have failed. So long as you keep in mind that it is the client who is the important person in the relationship, and your agency's work which is being done, then you are succeeding in your task.

Issues to think about

- How far is it possible to overcome an immediate impression of dislike for a client?
- What is the right course of action if you fall in love with/become obsessed by your client?
- Are you able to back down gracefully a) in life in general; b) in your voluntary work?

7 Working with professionals

You are not the only one involved

Whichever voluntary or statutory organisation you work for, your client may well be in contact not only with you but with members of one or more of the professions. He may be seeing doctors, social workers and teachers at the same time as he is seeing you. In some cases your involvement may be as a direct result of his contact with them, or it may arise as a result of referral from an entirely different source. It is therefore important to be clear where you stand not only in relation to your client but in relation to the other workers involved.

If you are to work effectively, it is necessary to be clear about how what you are doing fits in with what other people are doing. If you do not know where your job starts and other people's end, then there is always the possibility that you will work at cross purposes or duplicate effort. The result of this is that the client will not be as well served as he might otherwise be and may even be harmed by the confusion which he will witness and be affected by.

Issues to think about

- How far are you aiming to achieve the same results as professional workers in your field?
- How do you ascertain what those results are?
- What do you have in common with the professionals and where do you differ?
- What particular strengths does each of you have?

There are five main areas to think about when considering how you work with professionals. What follows aims to give you a useful framework in which to think about where you stand in relation to other workers.

Accountability

As an accredited volunteer working within an established organisation you are accountable to that organisation. You are also responsible for working in a way which will further its ends or achieve its aims. As a probation volunteer you may have a befriending role; as a volunteer working for Relate you may be offering mediation or counselling. But the professional workers your client is in contact with all have a different and sometimes even apparently conflicting involvement. This is despite the fact that the same circumstances may have led to your client's contact with you both.

Because the professional worker is accountable to a different agency, or because he or she holds a wider responsiblity within the organisation for which you both work as volunteers, the way each of you sees the job will be different. Also, the methods you both use may not be the same. Unless you are clear about this the situation can become confused, frustrating and dissatisfying in a way which will certainly not help your client. You need to know what you are doing and and how this is different from the tasks others are performing. Furthermore, you should be able to explain this to your client.

For instance, as a probation volunteer with a befriending role it is important to accept that it is part of a probation officer's job to exercise control. If you cannot accept this it will be hard for you to go on working with an officer if, for instance, he takes the client you have established such a good relationship with back to court for breaching his probation order. Your different jobs need keeping separate if you are to work successfully.

Similarly, couples who refer themselves to Relate may be in contact with lawyers or social workers. You may be working with the couple, or with the family as a whole, to help ease, explain, or restore relationships, or your task may be to allow partners to become reconciled to separation. At the same time, however, lawyers may be encouraging one or both of the partners to take up an adversarial stance in order to protect their legal rights. To complicate matters more, the social workers involved will be required to look primarily at the

immediate interests of the children in the family, regardless of
how adversely this may affect work going on with their
parents.

Once again, not understanding the differing responsibilities
placed on professional workers may lead to resentment,
annoyance and frustration. The important things for you to do
at this point are:

• identify which professionals you are likely to work
  alongside, given your chosen speciality
• compare their responsibilities and yours
• compare how best you can work, given the differences
  which will exist

Having done these three things you should be more clear, in
your own mind, where you stand. But you do need to take
account of other people. Ideally, therefore, you will need to
check with your clients and with the professionals involved
that they, too, have the same understanding of the divisions of
labour. If they do not, then at least the differences will be out
in the open.

Training and authority

Professionals, whether they are lawyers, doctors or teachers,
have undergone specialised training to equip them with the
skills, knowledge and expertise needed to offer certain services
in society. They are given responsibility for different aspects of
social welfare and because of their training and responsibility
they acquire some degree of authority. It is important for you
to be clear about the limits of that authority and what the
appropriate relationship is between the professional worker
and the volunteer. In this context it is useful to think about
some commonly accepted ideas of authority.

By authority we mean, in general, the power which people
are given the right to assume by others. If we accept that
someone has authority over us we accept that he or she has
the right to make certain decisions and act in certain ways, and
that it is not up to us to challenge this. In the context of
volunteer-professional relationships, therefore, we need to
consider where this right comes from and the areas over which
it extends. What follows is a brief account of the three main
sources of authority, and some equally brief suggestions about
the implications of these.

First, there is formal authority, where a lawyer has the power, because of certain rules and conventions, to represent the point of view or interests of someone in a law court or in a legal transaction. Another example might be where a medical consultant has the authority to make decisions concerning, first, the allocation of beds in a ward and, second, the treatment of the patients in them. The responsibility for performing certain tasks is established by law or administrative order. It is based on the possession of special knowledge, training and skill and the authority to make the relevant decisions follows on from this.

Second, there is a more generalised authority, which is related to social as well as professional status. Headmistresses often tend to become magistrates, bank managers are called upon to write character references and doctors find themselves becoming school governors. Because of their knowledge, skill and authority in one area of life they acquire authority in others. Their proven ability to exercise power tends to make them obvious candidates for other positions of power.

Third, as a volunteer you will undoubtedly come upon people who exercise considerable personal authority. Among professional workers, just as among other groups, there will be those who command a personal respect which accords them authority. It is not unusual for some family doctors to find themselves arbitrating family disputes, and the policeman may well find himself refereeing local football matches. Such people have often built up this authority and respect over a number of years during which they have established a reputation for sound judgement and considerable understanding.

It helps to clarify your relationship to the professionals you are in contact with if your bear these differences in mind. This is equally true whether your contact is face to face or indirect, through your client or organisation. At every stage you need to be clear whether the professional in question has ultimate responsibility in the situation in which you are involved. It may indeed be that a professional worker is responsible for your work, but it may not be. In fact he or she may have only limited knowledge of or authority in the area of work in which you are specialising.

It will also be important to consider the way, if at all, the professionals involved are responsible for, or to, your clients. Their involvement may be peripheral to the main concerns of your client if they are only involved for a short time while they provide a particular service in a quite small but clearly defined area of your client's life. Alternatively, a professional may be working as a key worker, charged with the responsiblity of co-ordinating a variety of services, seen by client and workers alike as essential.

Further, it will make a difference whether their authority results from the responsibilities they have been charged with, or as the result of habit or temperament. Some people, after all, have an authoritative way of talking even in areas where they have no responsiblity and very little expertise. It may be important both for your client, and for the working relationship between you and the professional, for you to consider whether an opinion offered has the authority of being his/her professional judgement, or whether it relates to a subject outside his/her expertise and has simply been offered in an authoritative way.

In the first case it may not be up to you to challenge or question the opinion, in the second it may be. The other possiblity, of course, is that it is your habit and temperamental deference towards professionals which has endowed the workers with powers outside their areas of expertise. It is important to recognise when you are doing this.

Issues to think about

- In what aspects of your work should you defer to the views of professional workers, and why?
- Whose views and judgements should take priority? When and why?

Nature and size of workload

Volunteers commonly feel that many professionals take only a cursory interest in clients. There is ample evidence that they can be brusque, impatient and pay only scant regard to the details which are so significant in distinguishing one client from another. Indeed, clients' assessments of the services they receive from professionals usually include reference to their satisfaction, or otherwise, as to whether they felt that they had been properly listened to.

The fact is, though, that a doctor may have 2,000, 3,000 or 4,000 patients on his or her books and the solicitor may be representing the interests of anything up to 10 people in the same court on the same morning. In these circumstances sheer numbers dictate that professionals cannot be interested in the people they are working for as entire and rounded personalities.

More significantly, professionals are not necessarily paid to involve themselves in the personal characteristics, feelings and idiosyncracies of their clients. These considerations are secondary for the professional. The nature of professional work involves focusing on a particular aspect of life, or a particular need, recognising a situation speedily on the basis of skill and past experience and acting effectively in a limited area. There is a sense in which the professional worker must see the individual as 'a case'.

For the trained and specialised professional the client is seen as one example of a type of person or situation about which there is a body of specialised knowledge. That is very different from the volunteer whose role is to act as a befriender. You are there to hear what the client has to say because he is who he is. It is his unique importance which is your concern, and your involvement may be precisely the result of the professional worker's acknowledgement that you have the time to listen while he or she does not.

Accepting that you and the professional are interested in different aspects of your client's life and have different jobs to do is one thing; deciding which is the more important is another thing entirely. The fact is that sometimes values clash and different people see different things as more important, and in these circumstances the client's view can sometimes be lost completely. In such a case your specialism is that you may know what your client thinks, feels and wants and can speak with some authority in this area.

Take, for instance, the old, infirm, confused man living by himself. Health workers, with what they regard as overriding responsibilities for the physical safety of their client, may see it as their job to exercise their considerable authority to remove someone from a situation which is clearly a threat to physcial safety or welfare. The social worker involved may agree, or may feel that the client has the right to retain his independence in his own familiar surroundings. Their legal or personal authority may come to bear at this point and the issue may be resolved without too great a weight being being placed on the views of the client, who may be rather easy to ignore.

You, in your role of befriender, may have a great deal of knowledge about the client's views and feelings. These should be made known, despite the fact that both the health worker and the social worker may be busy. It is not a foregone conclusion that the professionals' view must be overriding in this circumstance.

Issues to think about

- How do you make sure that professionals are informed of significant information and that they take your informed opinion into account?

Priorities

Not only are you and the professional interested in different things about your clients, you are usually in contact with far fewer people than a professional worker will be. For this reason you and the professional are likely to make different decisions about how long to spend with each client and in what order to do the work. Ideas of what will wait and what needs a great deal of time will vary. While this may be partly the result of the differing roles and responsibilities, it will also be affected by the pressure of time.

The policeman will devote more time and effort to the investigation of a crime if:

- it is a serious crime
- there is a reasonable chance of solving it and
- if evidence will be lost if speedy action is not taken

The Victim Support volunteer will ideally give what time is needed to the victim who is most seriously affected at the time he most wants that attention, regardless of how apparently 'trivial' the offence. These are two entirely separate priorities. If the policeman, the volunteer and the client can each accept the pressure the others are under everything may work out well. If they do not then there is ample room for friction. The distressed client fails to understand why 'his' burglarly does not seem to be receiving attention. The policeman may feel aggrieved that he cannot find the time to offer the support he would like to, and may even be irritated by the volunteer who does. The volunteer shares the client's frustration at being 'kept in the dark' by the police.

As someone working with clients who are often involved with professionals, you need to have some understanding both of the pressures imposed on professionals and of the way they deal with these in the organisation of their work. You need to understand this, not only for your own sake – to reduce your own frustration – but so that you can have realistic expectations and, if it is necessary, pass these on to your client. You could be wasting a great deal of your time, and possibly laying your client open to considerable disappointment, by fostering expectations which are unrealistic.

Of course, it is your job to support your client in his efforts to get what he sees himself as needing; but you are doing him no service by leaving him ignorant of the considerations which are likely to stand in the way of his getting what he wants. The facts may be that because of the housing shortage he is extremely unlikely to be rehoused, or that because of the pressure on hospital beds, despite his pain and social isolation, he can expect to suffer for many more years. Situations like these may make you want to launch a crusade. You should make sure that you know what can be done, and at what cost. You should also make sure that the cost is met by you and not by your client.

Issues to think about

- List instances of your own times of helplessness and defeat? How did you cope with them?
- How can you support a client who is having to face such helplessness and defeat?

Exchanging information

So far, while considering working with professionals, we have pointed to various differences in emphasis, expertise, authority and viewpoint which may separate them from volunteers. Finally, it is important to look at what the two can and should exchange in the way of information. What the professional knows about the client and what you as a volunteer know is likely to be considerably different. This raises new questions. What should you tell each other? What is relevant? What is important? What is confidential?

Perhaps confidentiality is the place to start. Depending on the nature of the work you are undertaking and the agency you represent, your client may tell you things in confidence on either the explicit or implicit understanding that you will not tell anyone else. In this case it is important to be clear right from the beginning whether the client is telling you, as an individual, or you as a representative of your organisation about those things he does not wish to have repeated. It may be best to make it very clear from the start that as a member of an organisation you regard the information he gives you as confidential to that organisation and not to you personally.

In whichever sense information is regarded as confidential, you and your organisation have to regard your client's right to privacy. As a volunteer working for Cruse, for example, you may learn a great deal about someone's financial difficulties, health problems or family disputes. You may feel that others could and would help if they knew, but it is not your right to disclose such information without the express permission of your client.

You might think it appropriate to point out the advantages of talking to the doctor or the lawyer or the social worker, but if your client does not agree, then that is the end of the matter. To use information about a person, even for what you see as his benefit, is to use that person. That has to be an abuse of the trust that was placed in you as a confidante.

Having said this it is usually acknowledged that there are some exceptions, where some considerations have even more importance than the individual's right to privacy. The exceptions to this general rule are normally considered to be cases where there is severe threat to the life or safety of someone who, because of his age or mental state, cannot look after himself. Young children and elderly confused people usually fall into this category. Although these exceptions are very rare, they are the ones which tax both professionals and volunteers greatly and so are perhaps worth giving some thought to here.

The trouble, of course, is that in these cases we all face the problem of making a judgement about a matter of degree. Principles are nice and easy – there are rules governing those; we use our heads and out comes the answer. But touch-and-go decisions about unique and individual people are far more difficult. On the one hand, we do not want to disclose information given in confidence. On the other hand, the cost of witholding information, which could save a life, is too high to allow for guesswork which amounts to little more than gambling.

Both professionals and volunteers can find themselves faced with the dilemma: suppose I say something and I am wrong – harm will follow. Or if I do not say anything, but my suspicion/feeling/information was right – harm will follow then, too. We may be talking here of circumstances which involve child physical or sexual abuse or mental cruelty, or the risks to the life or physical safety of the elderly and confused person. In our considerations, of course, we need some way of assessing the importance of how young the child is, how great the cruelty and how profound the confusion or handicap. In a nutshell, what we are thinking about is a matter of degree. Given that this person might be open to the possibility of harm at this time, how able is he or she to do something on his or her own behalf to stop this?

Issues to think about

- What do you do when you are in any situation where you are uncertain?
- How appropriate is your way of making decisions in your role as a befriender for those who may not be able to make decisions and exercise control on their own behalf?

In general, then, anything you are told in confidence you do not pass on without permission. It is important to remember that any professionals who are involved with the same client will be operating on the same assumption. Do not expect to hear detailed information which a social worker or a health visitor has acquired because of their special relationship with your client.

You may expect to hear, however, anything which affects your own safety in the situation. By the same token you should consider disclosing information which relates to the physical safety of others. If your client is seriously threatening violence to you or someone else – do say so.

There are other grey areas, though, which crop up more often. These involve pieces of information which it may well be appropriate and relevant to pass on and which are not strictly confidential. There will be details that you know simply because you and your client are alive in the world together.

Your client may not tell you that he is depressed or drinking too much. He may not even recognise this, but it may be obvious to you in just the same way that it would be obvious to a casual acquaintance, or someone sitting next to him on the bus. Someone, that is, who did not expect to share confidences at all. So do you tell the professional workers who are involved with your client? What is the difference between being a meddlesome gossip and working constructively in the interests of your client? Again, the distinction is not as clear-cut as it may seem.

The fact that something is true is not, in itself, sufficient reason for saying it. In this context the first thing to remember is that your client is the one who will decide whether you are meddling, so it is important to discuss with your client how significant what you think you know is. Find out if he gives it equal importance. Consider what the implications of telling someone else are. Why tell them? What will it do telling them?

An issue to think about

• Whose business is information about the client anyway?

How professional workers see you

In this chapter we have looked mainly at your attitude to professionals, how these are altered by your understanding of their situation and how this affects the three-way relations between you, professionals and your clients. It should at least be mentioned, though, that not all the decisions and understandings are within your control. It is more than likely that in some circumstances what you are able to do and how effectively you are able to operate will depend to a great extent on how the professional workers involved see you. Here are some possibilities.

Many professionals value voluntary organisations and the people who work for them for the competent and efficient way they work within well-defined areas, but this is not always the case. For some, people who are not professionals are amateurs, with all the implications of being semi-committed, semi-skilled and probably sloppy and unreliable. Along with this thankfully rare attitude goes the view that the volunteer, therefore, need not have too much time or consideration devoted to her views.

Issues to think about

• What ways can you find to establish that the opposite of 'professional' is 'unpaid', not 'amateurish'?
• Can you identify the circumstances where it is appropriate to insist on the authority and expertise which you, as a member of your organisation, have?

There is another misconception which a few professional workers may occasionally harbour, and which may pose difficulties for you. It is the combined view that a) the volunteer has all the time in the world and b) that it is not very clear what she is doing in the situation anyway. This view tends to lead to an invitation to make yourself into a general dogsbody.

Sometimes this is an invitation to waste your time. That is bad enough. Occasionally, and even worse, it may involve you

in being put under pressure to perform tasks which are
certainly not your business but which, for some reason, no one
else wants to take on. If the drain is leaking outside your
client's home this may well be of concern to you because it
concerns him. But beware. As a befriender it is not your job to
tackle the Environmental Health Department, even if all the
professionals involved quote the regulations and circumstances
which prove that it is not their job either!

Postscript

In this chapter we have looked at some of the ins and outs of
working alongside professionals. It may be an important part
of the work you are undertaking so it is worth getting it right.
We hope that by looking at some of the similarities and
differences between your approach and that of many
professionals we have been able to help you see your work in a
wider context. The point to be clear about is that you play a
significant part in the overall service your client receives. Be
clear and firm about what your work is – and what it is not.

8 Looking after yourself

Getting the balance right

Doing voluntary work is a little like falling in love. You make an initial commitment which you hope is going to work, but you can never be completely sure. It makes demands on you, some of which you are aware of from the outset, others you have to come to terms with as time progresses, or you may decide that you are not going to tolerate some of them. You do not know how long the relationship is going to last, perhaps for the rest of your life, perhaps for six months. As with falling in love, you hope that the relationship is going to be two-way, that what you put into it in terms of time and energy is returned to you in terms of fulfilment and a sense of purpose.

If you think of your life as a whole, one way of seeing it can be as a process of giving and receiving. Generally, if the two sides are balanced, life has a sense of satisfaction and achievement. When there is an imbalance, problems arise. If you are doing more giving than receiving you begin to feel drained, used and eventually burnt-out. Receiving more than you give may be acceptable for a while, but if the imbalance is over a prolonged period of time it eventually appears as guilt, resentment on the part of the giver, and frustration.

Your voluntary work is a part of your life as a whole. There are two ways in which you should check that there is a healthy balance between what you give and what you receive with regard to this work. The first is the relationship between you as a volunteer and the organisation for which you work. The second is between you as a volunteer and the rest of your life, with your other commitments and relationships.

Issues to think about

- In what areas of your life do you give more than you receive?
- In what areas of your life do you receive more than you give?
- Is there therefore an imbalance in your life? If so, what can you do about it?

You and the organisation

In any commitment to an on-going relationship there are often three stages to work through:

First stage

This is the 'honeymoon' period. You are fired up with enthusiasm and throw yourself into the new project, in this case, being a volunteer. You are willing to learn all that you can and you largely withhold judgement. There is a willingness to be influenced, to some extent at least, by the new people with whom you come into contact. Your new role takes up a large amount of your energies in two major ways. The first is the actual time that you spend on the organisation's business, and the second is the time you spend thinking and talking about your new experiences. It is a new factor in your life and therefore you may have to make adjustments to other parts of your life in order to accommodate it. For example, you see new significance in the things people say to you, or you re-examine beliefs that you have held for a long time in the light of your new experience. In short, you are an enthusiast.

Second stage

This stage is the period of disaffection, which can vary in length and severity. You will either work through it or you will extricate yourself from the relationship. It is a little like learning to drive a car. At first it is more or less just a car. Learning how to change gear and not crash into anything else is the most important thing on your mind, and occupies most of your thoughts. But once you have gained confidence and competence you begin to notice other things. The brakes are not as good as they should be, or the body rust is rather more rampant than you thought. As a volunteer in an organisation you begin to look around and notice its faults and limitations in addition to its virtues. You then have to decide whether to readjust your original enthusiasm so that you can accept the failings along with the virtues, or you decide that things were not as you thought they were going to be and you leave.

This is also the time when you compare how you function as a volunteer with how the other volunteers function. In the 'honeymoon' period you were aspiring to be like them and willing to learn whatever it took to achieve that ambition. But now there is a sense, in part at least, of having got there. You begin to assess your own abilities in the light of your new knowledge and experience gained from watching how the other volunteers work. You begin to experience the reality, without the first flush of enthusiasm, of just how much being a volunteer is going to cost you in terms of time and energy.

In many ways this period of disaffection, of seeing a distance between you and the organisation, is also the time when you need to be closest to it. You will need support, guidance and encouragement from the others involved. You may also need help in looking at your own achievements and what you can realistically expect for the future. If you are going to stay with the organisation, a sense of proportion needs to be maintained. This is so that you can acknowledge that some things are not as you expected or are happy about, but where you can also hang on to the positive, beneficial aspects as well.

Do not forget *why* you became a volunteer; if those reasons are still being met then you can probably work through this period of adjustment and go on to find fulfilment in the work. You may find that your original reasons for wanting to be a volunteer are not being matched by the work that the organisation is asking you to undertake. In this case, perhaps you need to think seriously about your future commitment. It may be that you can adjust your own needs and expectations to fit in with those of the organisation, or it may be that you need to look around for some other work that is more suited to you. If this happens, it is not a failure of either yourself or the organisation. Your time there will have taught you something, and altered your outlook to some extent, no matter how brief that time was.

Issues to think about

- What are the major areas of your organisation that you would like to see improved?
- What constructive ideas do you have to start the process of bringing about changes?

Third stage

This stage is one of consolidation. You have realised that you are an imperfect volunteer working for an imperfect organisation. However, there are still enough good and beneficial things both for yourself and your clients to encourage your continued commitment. This should not imply that you are willing to accept the status quo. You should still want to work to bring about improvements in yourself as a volunteer or in the way the organisation carries out its work. But you do accept that the things that need change are not enough to stop you being a volunteer. Indeed, the only way you can bring about improvements is by staying inside the organisation. Being a volunteer becomes a routine part of your life and the adjustments you once made to accommodate your role have simply become the way you order your time and energies.

Growing commitment

It would be pleasant if we could say that after you became an experienced volunteer you lived happily ever after. That, however, is rarely the case. When you are a new, relatively inexperienced volunteer, you are just another, albeit vital, cog in the wheel. But as you gain in experience you also become more involved in the running of the organisation. More responsibility is given to you, more decisions are expected of you, more difficult work is sent your way. You then come up against the age-old truism that no one can be all things to all people. The decisions you make or the changes that you implement are not always going to please everyone.

To put it bluntly, things can get pretty nasty. It is at times like this that you go home after your stint as a volunteer and wonder why you do it. Why do you put yourself through situations of unpleasantness or disapproval and leave yourself with feelings of anger or disappointment, frustration or hurt? This is again one of those times when, because you feel a distance between yourself and the organisation, you need to be closest to it. You need to seek the support and guidance of your colleagues and be able to talk through how you are feeling and why. You and your co-volunteers should give each other at least the same care and consideration that you all expect to give to your clients.

Growing cost

As your experience and confidence grows, so may your overall involvement in the organisation. You may find that being a volunteer is beginning to cost you more than you at first thought. You started off knowing that some clients would trouble or worry you, and you now find that your colleagues are doing the same. You need to remind yourself that you do have a choice in these matters, and it is not just a choice of whether to resign or not. Voluntary agencies, whether recently started up or long established, do tend to expect a lot from their volunteers, over and above the 'coal-face' work of dealing with clients. There are the administration, management, finances, and so on, to be seen to. Even who cleans the loo can be a problem.

As you became a reliable, experienced volunteer, the tendency will be to ask you to take on some of these additional tasks. You, who can see that somebody has to do these things, may feel a certain obligation to 'do your share'. You may even feel flattered that you have been asked. What you must bear in mind, however, is how these extra commitments affect the care or time that you give to the client, and how they affect your personal life.

You need to remind yourself that you can say no. Your value to the organisation should rest entirely on three things:

• how well you deal with the clients
• how supportive you are to the other volunteers
• how willing you are to further your experience and knowledge

All other commitments are additional extras which you should be free to choose whether you take up or not, without pressure or threatened disapproval.

The other problem is that you may want to say yes to everything that is offered to you. Increased involvement with the organisation increases your sense of fulfilment and achievement. In this case, you need to review your motives and performance at regular intervals. If you know that you are a good administrator but have doubts about the quality of the care you give to the clients, it would be easy to let the administration take over your time and commitment. We all tend to like doing what we know we are good at, even sometimes at the expense of what we should be doing. Or again, if you are a teacher, training new volunteers may be something that you can do with ease and confidence. But if that training in itself becomes more important than dealing with the clients, you have lost touch with the reasons why you are there in the first place. Eventually, this loss of a firm grounding could affect the quality of the training you give.

Ultimately, only you can decide what is the right level of commitment, regardless of how much or little you see other volunteers undertaking. It may be helpful occasionally to remind yourself of why you originally became a volunteer. Think about whether your reasons for doing the work are still the same and whether your needs are being fulfilled. If they are not, do you need to change some aspect of your involvement, or have the changes been good, positive ones for yourself, the client and the organisation?

Finding the right level

The commitment to being a volunteer tends to be an open-ended one. Unless you know that some change is going to take place in your personal circumstances, such as moving to another area in two years' time, you do not put a time limit on your involvement. The decision to leave may be made for you by, for example, an increase in other commitments in your life or failing health. It could be that it is a decision that eventually you will have to make for yourself. The most difficult decision to make is concerned with the recognition that you have gone stale. Five years ago you could sit with a very depressed client for three hours and be totally absorbed by what he was saying and feeling. Yesterday you were bored, felt you had heard it all before, were getting irritated with him, and felt you could be spending your time more usefully mowing the lawn.

If you were to listen to your favourite piece of music over and over again, it would eventually lose the qualities that, for you, made it so beautiful in the initial stages. The same can happen with your clients. The particular clients may change, but you remain the same in your approach to them. You listen, are attentive, sympathetic, tactful and so on. It is quite conceivable that at some stage you become bored with your own role, or that you have given so much to so many clients that there is very little left inside you to give any more. It takes some courage to admit this to yourself, especially as you can see other volunteers who have been going for 12 years without a hiccup. If you do not admit it, however, you could end up damaging both the clients and yourself.

It may be that you just need time away from the organisation for a while. It can be helpful to decide to take a long break, say three to six months, and not make a final decision until the end of that time. If you are straining at your leash in order to get back to the clients, your staleness was probably temporary and has cured itself, for the time being anyway. If, at the end or your break, the thought of getting back to work makes you yawn, it would probably be better to start thinking of other ways to spend your time.

Issues to think about

• What were your original reasons for becoming a volunteer? Are they still the most important reasons for staying a volunteer?
• When did you last say 'no' when asked to do something extra? How did/would you feel if you declined to do something when asked?
• How do you recognise when you have become stale?

Coping with change

The relationship between yourself and the organisation is one that is constantly changing, from both sides. You need to be aware of this and adjust your feelings and reactions accordingly. It is not enough to go on in the same old way, taking more and more on, doing the same things you have always done. To give the best service to your clients you have to give the best to yourself, which means not over-committing yourself and seeking support when you need it. You should examine your own feelings and motivation at regular intervals. You would not expect your car to give you its best performance if you did not replace the spark plugs and change the oil every so often. You need to treat yourself rather better than you might treat your car, and give yourself a service every now and again. Since you have undertaken to be a volunteer, you have an obligation to give the client the best care that you can, which in turn means looking after yourself to the best of your abilities.

You and your life

Throughout this book we have considered you in your role as a volunteer. Finally, we want to give consideration to you as a person, for whom being a volunteer is only part of your life. Perhaps we ought to restate here, as forcefully as we can, that unless you look after yourself and your own mental and physical welfare, you will not be able to give your clients the care and attention they need. Furthermore, you run a very great risk of harming yourself in the process if you try when you are not fit enough to try.

It could be argued that fully grown, fairly mature adults should not need telling how to look after themselves. Yet it is because we are adults and aware of the world around us that we tend to neglect ourselves. We do tend to take our responsibilties seriously, but sometimes in honouring those responsibilities we neglect ourselves for the sake of them. For example, the tired mother of two toddlers will push herself on for the children's sake; or, as we have discussed earlier, there is the carer who sacrifices her own needs and desires for the sake of an elderly or disabled relative. But the examples do not have to be so dramatic: take the volunteer who knows she will have to work long after midnight if she spends part of the evening doing her voluntary work; or the volunteer who carries on befriending an individual client even when her own life is raising difficulties. These all take their toll on a volunteer's resources. Once in a while they may not have any lasting effect, but if it is a pattern that is repeated too often, the effects can be lasting and debilitating.

Issues to think about

- List the last three times you gave yourself a treat.
- What were the last three times you let someone else do something for you, out of the routine and simply because they wanted to?

Being kind to yourself

If you have had difficulty answering these questions, perhaps you are not looking after yourself as much as you thought you were. Being kind to yourself is something that a lot of people find very difficult to do. It is often easier to be kinder to someone else – perhaps by giving time to a voluntary organisation? Yet you are the most important person in your life and you are the one who is in the best position to know yourself best. Therefore you are the best person to know how and when to be kind to yourself. Looking after yourself in an adult, mature way (even if that involves going off and flying your kite for an afternoon, as you did when you were a child), need not be careless self-indulgence. Rather it is a type of body-and-soul maintenance that is necessary if you are to continue functioning on the level that you want to function.

Another way in which you need to look after yourself relates to the fact that you probably do not exist in isolation. There are people around you whom you love and who love you. There will be times in your life when you receive from them more than, at that point, you are capable of giving back. But there will also be times when the reverse is true. Those are the occasions when you can support other people through difficulties and expect little in return, for the time being at least. But whatever your relationship, whether it be a spouse or partner with whom you live, or a friend with whom you share a fair amount of time and energy, the fact that you are a volunteer has its effect on the relationship.

It may be over-stating the case to say that this provides an imbalance in the relationship, but there can also be a tendency to under-play its significance. If your partner is a hard-working executive, you probably both make allowances for occasional irritability, and reluctance to have a late night during the week. Yet there can be a tendency to think that if you have had a hard time with a client, and you come home drained and irritable with tiredness, you should not make allowances for it. After all, the argument goes, it is only voluntary work. It does not actually pay the bills at the end of the month. Since it is 'only' voluntary, you have no right to let it affect your spouse/partner/friend. However, whether or not you are paid to do something has very little bearing on what it costs you to do it or on the value of your work. You should not devalue what you do or the effects it has on you simply because you are not being paid.

Learning to let go

In a number of organisations, the work that you do does have an element of confidentiality in it. This means that you will not be able to give a complete account of your experiences to anyone other than another volunteer or person involved with the agency. The result of this is that the people closest to you are automatically excluded from some significant part of your life. Hopefully, with experience you will be able to compartmentalise your life a little. This means that when you walk away from your client or organisation you can turn your mind to what you are going to, rather than hang on to what you have just left. Obviously there will be times when this will not be possible, for example, after you have been with a very distressed client. This is one of the reasons why it is so important to have someone within the organisation who is easily accessible and to whom you can talk. If you can talk things over freely with this person it will minimise how much of what you are feeling you take home.

None the less, if you are to survive as a volunteer and look after yourself in the best way possible, the understanding of the people important to you is vital. Going home and pretending that the day was marvellous when in fact you have spent four hours with a suicidal client is not the best way of ensuring your own well-being. It could also introduce tensions in your relationships that might otherwise be avoided.

Before becoming a volunteer there should be discussion between yourself and the most important people in your life. This should cover:

• what the confidential side of your work will mean
• how the other person will cope when you are upset by the clients
• how you keep a balance in your relationship when some of your time and energy is being invested elsewhere, albeit on a voluntary basis

When your commitment to the organisation increases, it should be discussed with your partner and his or her feelings taken into consideration. You will need the support of the people around you; you should not just assume it is there.

Issues to think about

• How has/will your work as a volunteer affect the people closest to you?
• What are your own three most pressing needs *now* and what are you doing to make sure that they are met?

Over to you

You have or will become a volunteer because you have something to offer other people, and in doing so you can gain fulfilment and satisfaction. We hope that this book will have made you think a little more deeply about some of the issues involved in being a volunteer and in giving support to other people. Giving yourself at least the same time and emotional energy as you would expect to give your clients is an important part of the process, and yet one that it is so easy to neglect.

Being with people who are in need or distress is never an easy thing to do. We hope we have helped you along the way a little and that what you give while being a volunteer is at least equally matched by what you receive.

Appendix Giving feedback

This book has asked you to consider some of the basic principles of listening and counselling. It has not been exhaustive and we recognise that in thinking about your answers to some of the questions we have posed you may have felt that more (or less) information or guidance would have been helpful. We would like to know what your reaction to this book has been, and what areas you felt were useful as well as those not so useful. Please also indicate if there are any particular areas we have not considered at all which you would have liked to have seen in the book, or any topics which you would like to read about in further depth.

1 What parts of the book did you find particularly helpful?
2 Were there any parts that were not helpful? Why?
3 Are there any topics which you would have liked included but which were not?
4 What parts of the book would you like to see considered in greater depth in the future?
5 Any other comments:

Please send your comments to: J. Ford and P. Merriman, c/o Bedford Square Press, 26 Bedford Square, London WC1B 3HU.

Further information

Useful addresses

The following is a list of some national organisations which use volunteers. For a comprehensive list of nearly two thousand organisations, consult *The Voluntary Agencies Directory 1991* (Bedford Square Press, 1990).

Abbeyfield Society
286/192 Darkes Lane
Potters Bar
Herts EN6 1AB
0707-44845
Accommodates lonely elderly people within the security and companionship of small households, befriended by a housekeeper who provides two meals daily. 600 local societies manage 1,000 houses, over 30 of which provide 'Extra Care'.

Age Concern England
National Council on Ageing
Astral House
1268 London Road
London SW16 4EJ
081-679 8000
Fax 081-679 6069
Provides elderly people with the help of over 250,000 volunteers who provide a wide range of services such as day care, visiting services, lunch clubs, over-60s clubs, and in some cases, specialist work for the physically and mentally frail.

Barnardo's
Tanners Lane
Barkingside
Ilford
Essex IG6 1QG
081–550 8822
Fax 081–551 6870
Helps over 18,000 children, young people and their families
through some 167 community-based projects.
Note: there are a number of divisional offices in England,
Scotland and Northern Ireland.

British Pregnancy Advisory Service
Austy Manor
Wootton Wawen
Solihull
West Midlands B95 6BX
056–42–3225
Probably the largest advisory service. Many branches provide
advice and counselling to over 40,000 people annually. Note:
there are numerous regional offices.

Cruse, Bereavement Care
Cruse House
126 Sheen Road
Richmond
Surrey TW9 1UR
081–940 4818
Offers national service of counselling for all who have suffered
bereavement. Has a Parents' Circle for widowed parents with
dependent children and also offers courses on counselling
before and after bereavement. House journal for its
volunteers: *Bereavement Care.*

National Association for One-Parent Families
255 Kentish Town Road
London NW5 2LX
071–267 1361
Offers help and advice to Britain's 975,000 one-parent families
and single pregnant women in raising children, housing, social
security, taxation, maintenance, appeals tribunals, etc.

National Association of Citizens Advice Bureaux
Myddleton House
115–123 Pentonville Road
London N1 9LZ
071–833 2181
Gives widest possible advice on almost all subjects. 7.1 million callers in 1989; considerable employment of volunteers.

Relate: National Marriage Guidance
Herbert Gray College
Little Church Street
Rugby
Warwicks CV21 3AP
0788–573241
Centres nationwide offer advice concerning any aspect of family life or of a personal nature, not just to couples.

Samaritans
17 Uxbridge Road
Slough
Berks SL1 1SN
0753–32713
Fax 0753–24322
Wide use of volunteers provide advice to suicidal and despairing people at all times of the day and night. Regional branches.

Victim Support
Cranmer House
39 Brixton Road
London SW9 6DZ
071–735 9166
Fax 071–582 5712
Provides volunteer support for victims of crime nationwide; more than 350 branches in the UK.

Volunteer Centre
29 Lower King's Road
Berkhamsted
Herts HP4 2AB
0442–873311
Provides information, training and support to any organisation or person working with volunteers in the public, voluntary or private sector. Wide range of publications, e.g. *Catalogue of Services*.

Statutory organisations

Social services departments and the probation service make extensive use of volunteers, also. They are organised on a regional basis throughout the UK and can easily be found in local telephone directories.

Publications

The following list is short, patchy and idiosyncratic. There are so many books on counselling and related subjects which you could go on to read that we hesitate to recommend any particular one. However, these are some of our favourites:

ELDRID JOHN.   *Caring for the Suicidal*, Constable, 1988.

GORDON, PAT (ed).   *Professionals and Volunteers – Partners or Rivals*, King's Fund, 1982.

KUBLER-ROSS, ELIZABETH.   *On Death and Dying*, Tavistock, 1987.

LONDON RAPE CRISIS CENTRE.   *Sexual Violence – The Reality for Women*, Women's Press, 1984.

MURGATROYD, STEPHEN.   *Counselling and Helping*, British Psychological Society and Methuen, 1986.

ROWE, DOROTHY.   Anything by her, but especially *Choosing Not Losing*, Fontana, 1988.

STORR, ANTHONY.   *The Integrity of the Personality*, various Penguin/Pelican editions.

Index

Other titles in the **Survival Handbooks** series:

Jane Brotchie
Help at Hand: The Home Carers' Survival Guide

Shirley Cooklin
From Arrest to Release: The Inside/Outside Survival Guide

Neil Davidson
Boys Will Be...? Sex Education and Young Men

Gingerbread/CEDC
Just Me and the Kids: A Manual for Lone Parents

Sandra Horley
Love and Pain: A Survival Handbook for Women

Tony Lake and Fran Acheson
*Room to Listen, Room to Talk: A Beginner's Guide to Analysis,
Therapy and Counselling*

Jacquelynn Luben
Cot Deaths: Coping with Sudden Infant Death Syndrome

Malcolm Macourt
*How Can We Help You? Information, Advice and Counselling for
Gay Men and Lesbians*

All books are available through bookshops. In case of difficulty, books can
be ordered by post direct from Plymbridge Distributors Ltd, Estover Road,
Plymouth PL6 7PZ
(tel. 0752-705251) adding 12½% to total value of order for post and packing
(minimum 50p).

For further details, please contact the Sales Manager, Bedford Square Press, 26
Bedford Square, London WC1B 3HU
(tel. 071-636 4066).

Room to Listen, Room to Talk
A Beginner's Guide to Analysis, Therapy and Counselling

Tony Lake and Fran Acheson

This book spells out simply and concisely what counselling, therapy and analysis do, and what they are there for. The guide includes interviews with people who have experienced therapy as clients, and with some of the increasing number of practitioners.

The authors, using material gathered originally for a BBC Radio 4 series of the same name, focus in particular on:

*   the growth of the therapy movement in the UK, and the reasons for its rapid expansion

*   what different forms of therapy have to offer, and how they work

*   what to expect if you are thinking of trying therapy for yourself, and what is required on both sides - from client and therapist - to make therapy work.

'I would recommend it to any counsellor who is uncertain about the boundaries between the three forms of therapy identified - counselling, psychotherapy and analysis.'   *CMAC Bulletin*

'This is a clear and readable little book which admirably fulfils its purpose.'
                                                                            Counselling, BAC

The Health Directory
Compiled for the 'Thames Help' programme by Fiona Macdonald

*In association with the College of Health
and the Patients Association*

A new edition of the former *Health Help* volume, first published by Bedford Square Press in 1987, the 1990/91 edition lists around 1,000 organisations set up to help patients and their families with many common (and not so common) health problems. They range from established national bodies such as the Red Cross and the NSPCC, to self-help groups dealing with a particular disorder.

Symbols are used to indicate when an organisation is a registered charity, has branches or local groups, welcomes volunteers or produces publications. The directory also includes organisations dealing with complementary medicine, ethnic minorities and general sources of help. The entries are listed alphabetically and in a comprehensive index by subject order.

The Voluntary Agencies Directory

The Social Activists' Bible

NCVO's directory of voluntary agencies is the standard reference work for anyone who cares about helping the community. It lists nearly 2,000 leading voluntary agencies, ranging from small, specialist self-help groups to long-established national charities. It gives concise, up-to-date descriptions of their aims and activities with details of

charitable status	local branches
volunteer participation	membership
trading activities	staffing

A list of useful addresses includes professional and public advisory bodies concerned with voluntary action; a classified index and quick reference list of acronyms and abbreviations give easy access to entries.

There is extensive coverage of groups concerned with women's issues, minority rights, self-help, community development and leisure activities, environment and conservation, campaigning and consumer affairs.

Voluntary agencies play an important part in making the world a better place to live in. This NCVO directory is the essential guide to their work.

'If you buy only one directory of voluntary agencies, buy this one and buy it every year.'   *Health Libraries Review*

'...an essential working tool.'   *Environment Now*

The Women's Directory
Compiled by Fiona Macdonald

The Women's Directory will enable women who wish to make contact
with others - whether for social, cultural, sporting, charitable, self-help
or political purposes - to locate and identify suitable groups and
organisations.   It refers women to appropriate 'umbrella' bodies,
whether voluntary, local-government-based or state funded, and gives
other sources of information about women's activities, including
relevant magazines and journals, publishers and bookshops. Presented
in an accessible, simple-to-follow format, with symbols used to give
additional information in the same manner as that outlined for *The
Health Directory.*

In addition to this book and other titles listed, **Bedford Square Press** publishes books on a range of current social issues. Series published include Survival Handbooks, Community Action, Practical Guides, Society Today, Directories, Reports, Organisation and Management, and Fundraising.

If you would like to receive a copy of the current catalogue, or further details of any title listed in this book, please complete the coupon below and forward it to:

> Sales Department
> Bedford Square Press
> NCVO
> 26 Bedford Square
> London WC1B 3HU
>
> Tel: 071-636 4066 (x2212)

☐   Please send me your latest catalogue/booklist (please tick)

☐   Please send me further details of the following titles:

     1. _____

     2. _____

     3. _____

     4. _____

☐   Please add my name to your regular mailing list. My areas of interest are (please state):

     _____

     NAME: _____

     ADDRESS: _____

     _____

     _____Post code: _____

(You may photocopy this page).